Faces of Kenya

DAVID KEITH JONES was born in Liverpool in 1933 and was a teacher at Brigg and Lichfield before going to Kenya in 1968 to teach physics. He started to publish photographs and articles on Kenya in 1969 and many of his photographs have been used in the Ministry of Tourism and Wildlife calendars in 1976 and 1977. He has lectured on photography at the School of Journalism, Nairobi University, has had photographs published in the Kenya Shell calendar in 1977, and is married with two children.

Faces of Kenya

David Keith Jones

SPHERE BOOKS LIMITED
30/32 Gray's Inn Road, London WC1X 8JL

First published in Great Britain
by Hamish Hamilton Ltd 1977

Copyright © David Keith Jones 1977

Published by Sphere Books Ltd 1982

Design by Patrick Leeson
Maps devised by the author and
drawn by Patrick Leeson

TRADE
MARK

Printed in Great Britain by
Fakenham Press Limited, Fakenham, Norfolk

For Carla

Contents

List of colour plates

9

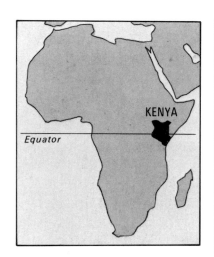

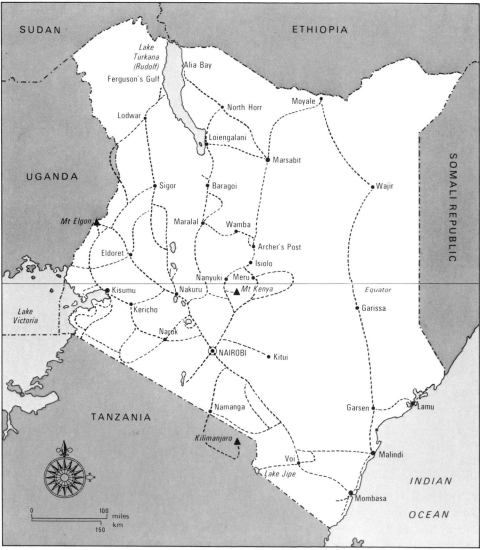

The Author's journeys in Kenya.

Introduction

W E OF THE 20th century increasingly cast glances over our shoulders, trying to catch glimpses of where we have come from, as we continue to accelerate our 'progress' towards we know not where.

In Africa there are still many people and places relatively unaffected by modern technology so that even now it is possible to reach out one's hand, so to speak, and touch the past.

To get the best from Africa it must be approached with humility, with the expectation of learning and enjoying the full sweep of Nature's spectacle and Man's versatility, ranging from coral reef to glacial mountain, from urban civilisation to hunter-gatherers. The whole of this spectrum may be seen in Kenya, whose great natural beauty provides a jewelled back-cloth which enriches an already important experience.

There are many—and increasing numbers of—20th-century people in Kenya, for the country is making rapid strides in education, technology, communications and agriculture. But this is a book about tracts of country so far only marginally affected by the present century, some of them because they are now National Parks and Reserves, others because they are still remote and difficult of access. Here we may see the wild animals for which Kenya is so justly famous, and also people who have knowledge and abilities of their own, attuning them to the great spaces in which they live.

As anthropologists have pointed out, 400 generations ago all our ancestors were hunter-gatherers and 400 generations are insufficient for any significant evolutionary change. So in a sense all the people in this book are ourselves, and are making use of skills which we could learn. And, equally, the pristine country which still exists in Kenya is the country we might have roamed had we not preferred to tame and ruin it.

I know that I am not alone in believing that in getting to know something of Africa one learns something of oneself. Hopefully these pages will evoke memories for readers who agree with me and, perhaps, prompt others to visit a beautiful region which may affect them at deeper levels than they anticipate.

A Gabbra woman leading her camel.

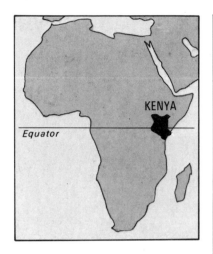

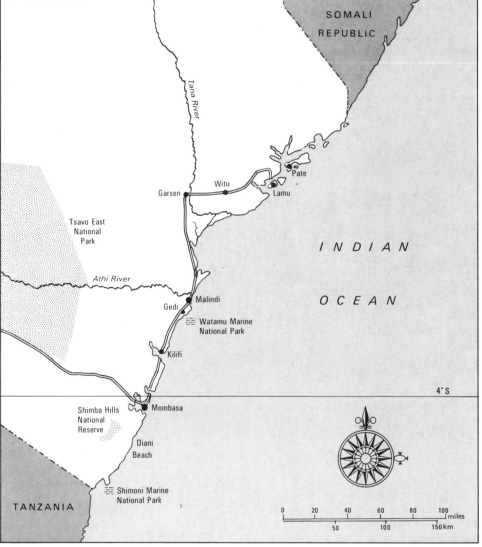

SOMALI
REPUBLIC

Tana River

Pate

Witu

Garsen   Lamu

Tsavo East
National
Park

Athi River

INDIAN

Gedi   Malindi

OCEAN

Watamu Marine
National Park

Kilifi

4° S

Shimba Hills
National
Reserve

Mombasa

Diani
Beach

Shimoni Marine
National Park

TANZANIA

0   20   40   60   80   100
                                           miles
       50   100   150 km

1 The Coast

Kenya itself is bisected by the equator but the entire coast is south of the line, the main town of Mombasa being 4° south. From the ocean end of the Somali border in the north to the Tanzanian border in the south is 270 miles as the crow flies, but bays, inlets and promontories give Kenya a mainland coastline of around 600 miles. About a third of this coastline has been developed as a holiday playground with tarmac roads and good hotels, most of them with beach frontages. In addition there are the islands of the Lamu archipelago at the northern end of the coast.

Although so close to the equator the climate is never excessively hot, being moderated by the south-east (Kusi) winds which blow from April to November and the north-east (Kaskazi) from December to March. The hottest season is from January to March when the mean maximum temperature is 91°F (33°C). The sea temperature is influenced by the South Equatorial Ocean Current and varies between 75°F (24°C) and 86°F (30°C). For a seaside holiday the climate is ideal and even in the rains, which usually occur around May (the 'long rains') and October or November (the 'short rains'), there are normally several hours' sunshine a day.

The largest town on the coast is Mombasa with a population of about 250,000. Situated on a small island, Mombasa is joined to the mainland by a causeway to the west, a suspension bridge to the north and a good vehicle ferry to the south. Mombasa is Kenya's main port and there is an international airport on the mainland about ten miles from the town centre.

North and south of Mombasa the coast is dotted with modern hotels but nowhere are the beaches crowded and in many places they are positively lonely. Most of the coast is protected by a coral reef; inside the reef the lagoons give safe, sheltered bathing at high tide and delightful pools full of marine life at low tide. Boat trips and dives amongst the coral are wonderfully worthwhile, whilst deep sea game fishing is popular from several centres including Malindi, a pleasant little seaside town 75 miles north of Mombasa.

Close to the town of Malindi there are two Marine National Parks—Malindi and Watamu. These Parks were established in 1968 and were the first Marine Parks in Africa. There is now a third Marine National Park at Shimoni, 50 miles south of Mombasa. All three Parks offer spectacular goggling and diving as well as trips in glass-bottomed boats over the coral gardens.

Inland, 22 miles south of Mombasa, the Shimba Hills National Reserve rises to 1,500 feet above sea level and gives good views of the south coast. Well known for its herds of

Sable and Roan Antelope this Reserve also has elephant and buffalo.

The fertile coastal strip varies between ten and twenty miles in width and is largely formed of old coral reefs. This narrow strip of land has a fairly good rainfall from the ocean; inland, the escarpment rises rapidly to the dry semi-desert nyika (dry bush) country which was such a barrier to early travellers. Most of the strip is now farmed, with coconuts and sisal much in evidence; but there are a few remnants of the coastal forests left at Jadini on the south coast and the Sokoke–Arabuko Forest to the north. Here there is a wealth of butterflies and birds, including some species unique to these areas.

The Kenya coast has an ancient history; settlements have been recorded by ancient writers and travellers as early as A.D. 150. Malindi was thriving when Vasco da Gama—the first European to visit this coast—placed his cross there in 1498. Traces of this long history can be seen in Mombasa itself where Fort Jesus—built by the Portuguese in 1593—is now a National Museum. Ocean-going sailing dhows from Arabia visit the Old Port each year in March and April as they have done for at least 2,000 years. There is another National Monument at Gede, near Malindi, with the well-excavated remains of an Arab town founded around 1300.

Further north still are the delightful islands of the Lamu archipelago where there are many interesting ruins. Lamu town is a unique survivor of a bygone age, its narrow streets still devoid of cars.

The coastal people come from varied backgrounds. Over the centuries the original Bantu population has been supplemented by people from Arabia, Persia and, more recently, Asia. A large number of the present population are Muslims, over 40 per cent of Mombasa's residents being of this faith. The non-racial character of Islam has resulted in a good mix of ancestry. Although purdah is not as strict today as in the past the vast majority of Muslim women still wear their black 'buibui' out of doors.

South of Mombasa the village people are mainly of the Digo tribe whilst to the north the largest group is the Giriama. The Giriama used to live in fortified settlements called Kaya, many of them quite large. They were usually on a hill top and some are still remembered as sacred places. Many of the traditional ways survive and visitors to Kenya's coast will see their grass-thatched houses and dug-out canoes.

Friendly people and a near-perfect climate; huge unspoilt beaches sheltered by coral reefs, alive with tropical fish; groves of palms rustling in the monsoon breeze; such is the coast of Kenya.

An old woman of Lamu; the nose ring contains a herbal charm.

IN A LAND of deserts and lakes, snow mountains and coral reefs, volcanoes and hot springs, wild beasts and exquisite birds, any starting point is arbitrary.

Let us begin with a warm evening on a small island where many early visitors made their first contact with Africa.

There are ten thousand people sitting in the square. In the narrow streets leading up the hill figures sit in every doorway, shadows spilling out into the night. Quiet talk fills the soft air with a murmuring confidence and towards the top one street is blocked by women, black-hooded in the total mystery of their buibui.

In front of the Mosque the throng is divided; men in white skull caps and kanzus, some holding their baby sons, sit on the warm, dry ground separated by a roped pathway from the anonymous, dark sea of women. The Riydha Mosque is decorated with lights and from its balcony come the high, compelling, chanting prayers that call forth the responses from the multitude. This is the climax of the ziara, or festival, to celebrate the Prophet's birthday, the most important of the many ziaras held on Lamu Island. Towards midnight the crowd rises and holy water is sprinkled on everyone. There is no rush as the thousands move off through the maze of streets, only a quiet, intimate murmuring as we all stroll to our beds.

Earlier, in the afternoon, the same open space was thronged with carnival crowds to see the many dances and enjoy the strong, vital music. In the Goma dance men with sticks, wearing kanzus, formed two sides of a rectangle and rocked rhythmically in time with their chorus master who chanted a song; whilst in the centre dignified gentlemen performed a ritualistic sword dance portraying the traditional rivalry of the two halves of the town. Near the Mosque a group of younger men showed off their prowess and strength in the Kirumbizi dance as they slashed at each other with staves. The square was filled with varied groups of dancers, each with its clustered audience, the clumps of young women taking the chance to prove that the flicker of dark eyes through the slit of a buibui can be as enticing as more open wantonness.

Here in this square the visitor is made conscious of something he will notice throughout the whole country; the enduring values and traditions of pre-20th-century Africa. For the town of Lamu is the best preserved example of an urban way of life which has lasted at least ten centuries, and which is unique to this coast.

Many visitors have labelled these coastal towns Arab or oriental but this is mistaken. A number of facts suggest that, although like seaboard civilisations everywhere, they absorbed influences and people from abroad, these towns were essentially local and African in character. The side-blown horn or siwa for example is a style of instrument that occurs throughout Africa from coast to coast, but not elsewhere. The siwa of Lamu, cast in brass by the lost-wax process, and that of Pate carved in ivory, are both over two hundred years old and are magnificent pieces of craftsmanship. In Lamu drums are beaten with sticks and with the heel of the hand, something which is never done in the East. Swahili is a Bantu language. The architecture is unique to this area and has special points of beauty, notably the quality and

Left:
Shela Mosque at the east end of
Lamu Island.

Coconut Palms.

A corner of the old town,
Mombasa.

design of the plasterwork decorations which are of a type not found in any other culture.

The town of Lamu has existed on its present site for at least 600 years and has had periods of great wealth and elegance, as have many other towns on the Kenyan coast. The first Portuguese visitors were astonished by the wealth of this region and described the silk of Pate Island (only ten miles from Lamu) as the best they had ever seen. Beautiful pieces of this silk, heavy with gold thread, still survive but sadly most of the jewellery has been lost. All the refinements of civilisation were there: poetry, dance, carved furniture, elegant costume. The sanitation was especially fine at a time when European arrangements were disgusting. Today Lamu is no longer rich, but when walking the narrow streets and spacious squares of the town one imbibes a strong sense of the past. Old buildings and rhythms remain and modern life and the motor-car are kept at bay. Changes there have been but there are still old ladies wearing golden jewellery and the sailing boat is still the main means of transport. Crossing the channel from the mainland to Lamu, passing the ocean-going sailing dhows from Arabia, climbing the steps on the waterfront, one is crossing the centuries and re-entering the world which the first European sailors found when they visited this coast five hundred years ago. Lamu and the ruins of other coastal towns are important because they remind us of something which many Westerners have too studiously ignored: that here in this land has grown and flourished a vast variety of ways of life with individual strengths and beauties of their own. If you are a city dweller it will do you no harm to realise that this tract of Africa which has cradled the elephant and some of the oldest human bones yet known has also nurtured a small but unique urban civilisation which was thriving before Marco Polo went to China.

How Lamu and the other coastal towns became rich is not completely known; certainly trade must have been important

A street scene in Lamu where even today vehicles are not allowed.

and it has been suggested that Lamu had access to large numbers of money cowries, the shells which were currency throughout East Africa and which even today are valued ornaments in parts of Kenya over five hundred miles from the coast. Certainly if the islanders had been able to fish cowries in large numbers from their own waters it would have been the equivalent of owning your own private mint today. But, however acquired, their undoubted wealth enabled them to make the best use of the available building materials.

From coral they cut blocks of coral rag to build a town of narrow shady streets on a plan which drained even the monsoon rains with ease. The roofs were supported by beams of hardwood from the mainland covered with sandstone and coral. This made the roofs so heavy that the rooms were perforce long and narrow. Clever proportions and beautiful plasterwork gave these narrow rooms a feeling of spaciousness far in excess of their actual size. The high standard of architecture and design was at its best in the bathroom and toilet arrangements. Many houses had three or four bathrooms with drainage into pits deep in the sand, placed far from wells. These bathrooms were decorated more elaborately than the rest of the house with plasterwork and sculptured coral. The tank which stored water for bathing, fed in many cases by a conduit from outside, contained small fish chosen to keep down the mosquitoes. Some houses had two tanks, one of which was heated from outside to give hot water.

All this was two hundred years ago and has been lost for ever. But the large open squares still are an integral part of the life of the town, acting as meeting place, theatre, church and drawing-room. In the narrow streets the carved doors became a symbol of good taste and wealth and the sense of design produced many types of sailing boat special to the island.

Although Lamu is the only remaining town of the coast civilisation there are many villages which still have their legacy of songs, dances and traditional festivals. These occasions bring to life the very spirit of the past, the strong tunes and melodic rhythms evoking scenes which must have made towns like Gedi vital places to live in. Today the ruins of Gedi, ten miles south of Malindi, are a National monument with the same status as a National Park. Founded around A.D. 1300 Gedi was a walled town similar to many others on the coast; the present ruins date from the 15th century when the population was about 2,500. No one knows for certain what destroyed Gedi, only that the city was abandoned in great haste. Now the charming ruins snuggle in the shade of great forest trees to remind us of a culture hidden in the past.

Present-day Mombasa is modernised almost beyond recognition. The splendour of the old city with its fine stone houses, high standards of craftsmanship and riches of copper, silk and gold has gone for ever; but a few streets and buildings near the Old Port offer a hint of the past. For a few months each year, between February and April, the visiting dhows from Arabia give the old harbour something of its former atmosphere. The mariners who sail these vessels are themselves the last survivors of a way of life which stretches back into pre-history. These sailing dhows make use of the monsoon and trade winds which will still be blowing when the last iron ship has foundered and the last drop of oil has burned.

The Arab sailors never use the word dhow, which may come from the Swahili 'dau' in general use in the 19th century to describe a sailing boat. The most common type of dhow today is the Boom which can displace as much as 300 tons. They are attractive craft, narrow at both ends, and thus representing the oldest maritime traditions of the Persian Gulf. It was not until the Portuguese sailed these waters that the Arabs started to copy them and build boats with square sterns like the smaller Sambuks. But the Portuguese brought more with them than a new way of building boats and it is no coincidence that the old harbour is dominated by Fort Jesus, the 16th-century Portuguese fort, now a National Museum and symbol of the new forces and changes which Europe introduced to Africa.

In contrast many people of the coastal tribes keep alive other more ancient ways of life. It is an interesting fact that the traditions of rural Africa have survived more successfully than those of the coastal towns. For the urban civilisations are now only represented by Lamu, whereas many tribes along the whole length of the coast preserve some remnant of their old ways, both within a few miles of Mombasa and close to the main roads.

The Giriama, for example, continue to build grass houses, fashion dug-out canoes, enjoy their coconut-palm wine and fish; and their women can still be seen at sunset bearing water from the wells in gourds, balanced delicately on their heads. Undisturbed by modern crises these people have an intimate contact with the natural beauties of the coast. In their dug-out canoes the fishermen explore the fantastic world of coral reef and lagoons, catching fish which are extravaganzas of colour and design.

Narrow streets like this one on Lamu Island date from the 18th century.

An old lady of Pate island wearing traditional, finely worked, gold earplugs. The nose ornament is made from an 1851 American gold dollar.
Right:
This *Siwa*, or side blown horn, is a new one but follows an old tradition. When Vasco da Gama visited the Kenya coast in 1498 the King of Malindi showed him two made of ivory.

Lamu waterfront in April with two ocean-going
Booms. These ships can displace up to 300 tons
and, being narrow at both ends, represent the
oldest maritime traditions of the Persian Gulf.

Right:
Digo fishermen in a dug-out canoe, south of
Mombasa.

Siyu Fort is in the centre of Pate island, north of
Lamu. It was originally built early in the 19th
century.

Visitors too may enjoy these pleasures in the National Marine
Parks where you do not need to be an expert swimmer to enter
the gorgeous world of the tropical fish. The whole coast is a feast
for the sense of vision. Sea, coral, sky, flowers and birds, all show a
brilliance of shades and hues to delight the eye. But the coast is
merely an appetizer—preparation for the greater riches which lie
inland. Coastal visitors should drive to the Shimba Hills National
Reserve, the only place in Kenya where they will see the grace of
the Sable Antelope. The glossy black males with dapper white
face markings are perhaps the finest of the antelopes; with their
magnificent scimitar horns they have been known to kill lions.
Lions exist in this Reserve but they are very rarely seen and
although evidence of elephant is abundant they too spend most of
their time in the forest.

But these hills are a splendid vantage point; from here we may
look back towards the coast and the gleam of the blue sea; or we
may turn to the west where the huge mystery of the continent
beckons us. What a moment this must have been in the old days
when the only way into Africa was on foot; to climb the first
coastal hills, turn one's back on the ocean and begin the long trek
into the hinterland.

The treasures, inside the continent, which justified this act of
faith have been pillaged for centuries; but the remnants which
survive today will more than justify our own journey into this
rugged, varied land that teems with life like no other place on
earth.

22

Local fishing boats or *Jahazis* at low tide on Lamu Island; even now most travelling is done by boat.

Mandhry Mosque, founded in 1570, is the oldest of Mombasa's many Mosques.

This Malindi mosque is modern but the pillar tombs with their phallic symbols are ancient; the taller one dates from the 15th century. Tombs like this are found only in East Africa.

The *Goma* dance is part of the celebrations of the Birthday of the Prophet — the *Maulidi al Nebi* — held on Lamu Island. It is the biggest Muslim festival in East Africa.

This young woman has the face markings typical
of the Giriama people who live on Kenya's coast
to the north of Mombasa.

The *Zumari*, or Swahili oboe, gives a haunting,
plaintive song.

The 'scissor dance' is performed at weddings.

A drummer in a coastal village.

Muslim women watching a dance in the village of Witu.

A young woman of Lamu with
the typical buibui dress of
coastal Muslim women.

Hands and drums.

33

The walled city of Gedi was founded in the late 13th century and suddenly abandoned in the early 17th century. This is the entrance to the Palace with the Pillar Tomb in the background.

16th-century Fort Jesus was built by the
Portuguese (who employed an Italian architect). It
is now a National Museum.

A Giriama fisherman with his
dug-out canoe.

Ocean-going dhows in the Old Harbour at Mombasa.

Old friends on Lamu waterfront.

Dried fish are popular in coastal markets.

Morning on Lamu waterfront.

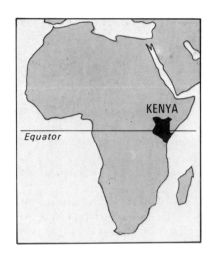

KENYA

Equator

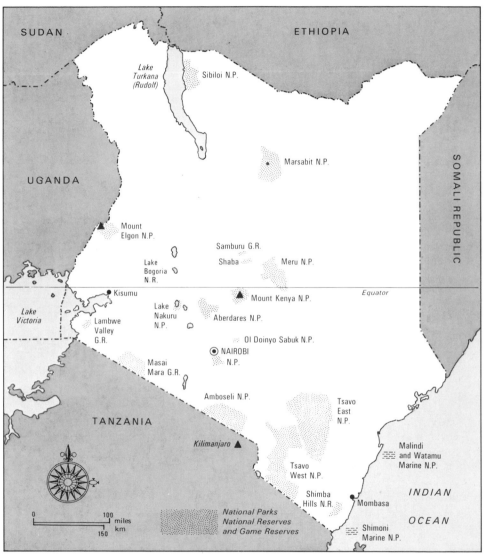

SUDAN

ETHIOPIA

Lake Turkana (Rudolf)

Sibiloi N.P.

SOMALI REPUBLIC

UGANDA

Marsabit N.P.

Mount Elgon N.P.

Samburu G.R.

Shaba

Meru N.P.

Lake Bogoria N.R.

Kisumu

Mount Kenya N.P.

Equator

Lake Victoria

Lake Nakuru N.P.

Aberdares N.P.

Lambwe Valley G.R.

Ol Doinyo Sabuk N.P.

⊙ NAIROBI N.P.

Masai Mara G.R.

Amboseli N.P.

Tsavo East N.P.

TANZANIA

Kilimanjaro ▲

Malindi and Watamu Marine N.P.

Tsavo West N.P.

INDIAN

Shimba Hills N.R.

Mombasa

OCEAN

0   100   miles
                   150   km

National Parks
National Reserves
and Game Reserves

Shimoni Marine N.P.

44

2 Game Country

Over 13,000 square miles have been set aside in Kenya as National Parks and Game Reserves where the wildlife is protected. These range from the snow-clad summit of 17,058-feet-high Mount Kenya to the coral reefs of the Marine Parks, and contain, between them, the majority of species native to Africa.

The largest of these Parks is Tsavo with an area of just over 8,000 square miles. Halfway between the coast and Nairobi, Tsavo is divided by the road and railway into two halves, Tsavo East and Tsavo West.

Tsavo East, huge and dry, is famous for its large elephant population still close to 10,000 in spite of heavy poaching in the mid-1970's. During the droughts of the early 70's the elephant cleared large areas of bush which has reverted to grassland and attracted plains game such as zebra, impala and buffalo. Tsavo West, hillier and more green, also has large herds of elephant together with a vast variety of ungulates and predators. Vehicles must keep to the roads, but there are over 1,000 miles of these in the Park and good game viewing is a virtual certainty.

Further west, Amboseli National Park is at the foot of 19,340-foot Kilimanjaro, Africa's highest peak. When the mountain is clear this must be the most scenic Game Park in the world. Here, a great variety of animals congregate around the springs fed by Kilimanjaro's snows. Very good game viewing is to be expected because of the short grasses of the region. Elephant, lion and cheetah are normally easy to find. Giraffe, zebra, buffalo, Grant's and Thomson's Gazelle are practically guaranteed. Rhino can still be seen occasionally.

Still further west, the Masai Mara Game Reserve is the only place in Kenya where animals may be seen in the vast numbers which were commonplace throughout the country only eighty years ago. Particularly famous for its lions, the Mara is the only Reserve where visitors are free to drive off the roads. The heavier rainfall of this area ensures that the grass recovers quickly from vehicle damage which might be more serious in a drier area like Amboseli.

To the north of Mount Kenya, Samburu Game Reserve straddles the Uaso Nyiro river and again has a vast variety of game. In this dry area Grevy's Zebra, Reticulated Giraffe and Beisa Oryx can be seen along with the more usual elephant, buffalo and lion. Crocodile are a feature in the river whilst dramatic rock peaks add interest to the scenery.

East of Mount Kenya, Meru National Park is very well watered by Kenya's largest river, the Tana, and a myriad other streams.

Further north again is Mount Marsabit National Reserve, a range of forested, volcanic hills, isolated in a sea of deserts. Here some of the largest elephants left in Africa can be seen and the rare Greater Kudu is easier to find than elsewhere.

In the extreme north of Kenya, on the eastern shores of Lake Turkana, the Sibiloi National Park contains the world's largest concentration of crocodile and herds of Tiang and Zebra. This is the only large sanctuary which does not offer accommodation. Visitors to this remote and difficult area must be completely self-contained.

These are the main game viewing areas but in addition there are the Mountain National Parks, where there is plenty of game in the forests, and a number of small National Parks which have been established to protect a particular species or area.

There are also large tracts of Kenya outside Parks and Reserves where vast numbers of animals still roam; wildlife is protected throughout the Republic where a total ban on hunting was imposed in 1977.

Most of the Parks and Reserves have between 80 and 100 species of mammals, not to mention the reptiles. The avifauna is astonishingly rich with more than 400 species recorded in many areas.

With such a wealth of wildlife available, most visitors try to see too many areas. Journeys can be long and tiring and it will often be more rewarding to stay in one Park or Reserve for several days instead of trying to be in a new Park every night.

Climate in the game areas is decided mainly by the altitude. Sibiloi, at 1,200 feet, is the hottest, followed by Tsavo East. The Masai Mara is at rather more than 5,000 feet and is probably the coolest of the Game Reserves—leaving aside the very high Mountain Parks.

Most of the larger Parks and Reserves offer three levels of accommodation in luxury lodges, self help cottages (or bandas) and camp sites for self-contained campers. Marsabit and the Masai Mara have no bandas and Sibiloi is for campers only.

One of the smallest of Kenya's 20 wildlife sanctuaries is also one of the most famous. Nairobi National Park is only four miles from the city centre and yet has over 80 species of mammals and more species of birds than the whole of the British Isles. 44 square miles in area, Nairobi Park is fenced on the city side but unbounded to the south. Animals are free to come and go and there are big movements depending on the rains. In dry weather the animals congregate in the Park to benefit from its many dams and streams. At these times the Park may carry tens of thousands of animals and the only large mammal missing is the elephant. As a forctaste or a farewell glimpse this small Park is ideal; but only the larger sanctuaries can really give the true taste of Africa.

This elephant has just blown a trunkful of dust over himself, a habit said to protect the animal from parasites and flies.

WE ALL KNOW, in an academic sense, that man as a species has existed for a very long time and that we have only emerged with our present dominance in the comparatively recent past. The game country of Kenya puts this piece of knowledge into context and enables us to experience it at the deep, intuitive, personal level where all knowledge is felt as well as known. When something is learnt in this deep sense the knowledge becomes part of ourselves and enriches our lives.

In Kenya's thousands of square miles of game country man is not yet the dominant animal and hopefully he never will be. In this remaining wilderness, given time to soak it in, one can finally come to grips with the fact that for around half a million centuries mammals have been the dominant form of life in Africa and that only in the last of these centuries has man become the dominant mammal.

A few figures will help to make the point. On 7 June 1905 young Captain Meinertzhagen was marching from what is now Kitale to Nandi Fort in western Kenya:

'On the march back from Quitale I counted 124 giraffe, 232 topi, 167 Jackson's haartebeeste, 17 bushbuck, 85 waterbuck, 24 oribi, 4 rhino, 7 warthog, 62 Chapman's zebra, 27 ostrich, 14 kori bustard and 4 lion in a little over 10 miles.'*

Today this area is a network of roads and tracks and is almost entirely under cultivation. True, it contains the remnants of the Nandi and Kakamega forests but even these are rapidly being turned into charcoal and paper. I have driven over many roads in the area and walked the Nandi Hills without seeing any game. There are a few giraffe left on the high land between Kitale and Eldoret; the remaining antelope are rare and shy; the rhino and the lion have definitely gone. It is the same over vast tracts of Kenya; where seventy years ago there was an abundance of animals today you will find almost nothing.

Only in the best of Kenya's National Parks and Game Reserves is it now possible to get somewhere near Meinertzhagen's figures. Perhaps it is easiest in the Masai Mara where in a ten-mile drive before breakfast in February, 1975, my wife and I were able to count 287 topi, 181 gnu, 99 impala, 80 Thomson's gazelle, 67 elephant, 66 zebra, 40 baboon, 38 giraffe, 20 hippo, 17 waterbuck, 9 buffalo, 6 lion, 5 mongoose, 3 warthog and 2 rhino. This is no more than a casual observation made without binoculars on a day when the main aim was photography; but it may serve to emphasise the feeling of Nature's triumphant abundance that such a morning brings. The early European visitors were so overwhelmed by this abundance they thought it inexhaustible; and so they plundered it. Today's Parks are only a remnant of the original splendour; but they are still vast enough to enable us to recapture a past which having lasted millions of years has all but slipped out of our reach in one man's lifetime.

Amboseli is a good place to start. The short grass makes it easy to get unobstructed views, the animals are used to cars, and there is the splendid backdrop of Kilimanjaro rising 16,000 feet above

* *Kenya Diary* (London, 1957).

These handsome Beisa Oryx are found in northern Kenya. They are specially adapted to arid conditions being able to go for long periods without water. Their body temperature rises considerably during the day—a mechanism which ensures that they do not need to evaporate water to keep cool.

the plain only 25 miles away. The plains of Amboseli are so extensive that animals are hidden by the distances and, driving across them, one gradually becomes aware of far-off specks which later realise themselves into herds of wildebeeste or zebra, Grant's gazelle or elephant. One morning our first excitement was a herd of 25 elephants, tightly grouped and moving purposefully across the open grasslands towards a distant swamp. It was a herd of females and calves, some very young, and they seemed to draw in towards each other as we approached. There is something inexorable about a herd like this moving across country. No browsing, no pausing to pluck branches or bunches of grass, no moving this way and that. Instead a steady marching, the young ones trotting to keep up. Other animals do not deflect them; they stride majestically, as though conscious they are invulnerable, and all give way before them. Moving like this against the back-cloth of Kilimanjaro they make a powerful and beautiful scene, its drama so unquestionable it sweeps away reservations about hackneyed postcards.

Many visitors and scientists find elephants the most interesting animals to observe. There is the constant feeling that the elephants too know something, understand, make decisions, have feelings, contacts, friends. Stories of elephants are legion, many of them very well authenticated. Modern hunters say elephants know the boundaries of the National Parks and will smartly step inside when hunters are around. Would that the poachers knew the rules and stuck to them as carefully as their victims.

A number of cases of elephants aiding an injured comrade have been recorded by hunters and mother elephants have been seen to carry a dead baby around for several days. It has been known for a hunter to track a wounded elephant only to come on the corpse minus tusks, these having been broken off and smashed by his companions. Thanks to Simon Trevor's wonderful film it is now common knowledge that wild elephants coming on a skeleton of one of their own kind will fearfully examine the bones, carry them away, and scatter them far and wide, although they will ignore the remains of other animals.

As well as being the biggest and in some ways the most interesting of the animals, elephants are in a sense the most tragic. A century ago they were the masters in the land. Of course they have been hunted for centuries, but like no other animal they had the run of the continent, went where they chose, migrated when they felt like it and generally managed their own affairs. No other large animal has such a wide range of habitat, from 12,000 feet in the mountain forests through savannah and semi-desert bush to the coast. Eighty years ago elephants visited what is now the centre of Nairobi and have been seen on the city's racecourse in the early days. They used to cross the Kavirondo Gulf of Lake Victoria, before Kisumu was thought of, walking on the shallow bottom of the lake, breathing through their upraised trunks, like snorkels.

In 1903 Meinertzhagen saw an elephant migration near Nyeri, now a prosperous town:

'Creeping up a small gully, I found myself but 60–80 yards off

This family group of females and calves is crossing the Uaso Nyiro river in Samburu Game Reserve. Female elephants remain together all their lives but will drive males out of the group when they become sexually mature at the age of about twelve years.

Left:
The Masai Giraffe can reach a height of 18 feet which makes him the world's tallest animal.

The leopard is by far the most elusive of the big five and many visitors will not have the luck to see one. Nocturnal, solitary and cunning, they manage to survive in places where other game has been exterminated. Even in heavily populated rural areas of Kenya occasional leopards are still troublesome, taking sheep, goats, dogs and chickens. In the past this would have resulted in a spear hunt by every able-bodied male, with great honour to the first man to plant his spear. Nowadays they are normally trapped in baited cages and released in a National Park or Reserve—an exercise that has resulted in injuries to more than one of Kenya's dedicated National Park Wardens. A number of lodges regularly bait an adjacent tree in a bid to give their guests a good view of leopard; to see one in the wild without baiting is good luck indeed.

this huge stream of moving elephant, going very slowly, sometimes in groups of eight or ten, sometimes two or three together and an occasional solitary beast; lots of calves; and to right and left I could see no end to the moving mass, each following on the other's trail. I tried in vain to count them, for the head of the column was in the far distance and the tail was approaching me, but I should say there must have been about 700 animals. They were moving at a steady walk, not feeding; the last beasts to pass me were a cow and a very small calf, and the rear of the column was level with Nyeri Hill as the sun rose behind Mount Kenya. I shall never again see anything like that.'

Neither will you or I, for the elephant has been cleared—exterminated—from large areas of Kenya where he has previously been free to roam for all the 50,000,000 years since the first apes and monkeys began to evolve.

For such a large important animal to be removed from many areas and confined to others in the space of one man's lifetime is cataclysmic in environmental terms, and no one has much idea of the long-term effects which this will have on either the land or the elephants themselves. On the one hand there is the fear that heavy poaching and a shrinking habitat will make the elephant extinct. On the other there is the problem of elephants, newly confined to areas they would normally have merely moved through, increasing in numbers, destroying the trees, altering the nature of the vegetation like no other animal (with one exception) can. Some say the numbers should be culled, others that they should be left to themselves to find a 'natural balance'—in an unnatural situation. The scientists are in disarray for although there are dedicated and capable men working on elephants there are not enough of them and they do not yet have firm answers. How can we have any answers? Our time-scales are too short, our experiments are too small. Have the elephants been 'farming' Africa for millions of years, knocking down trees and creating grass-lands which then revert to bush and finally to trees again, many decades, perhaps centuries later? Or are the new grass-lands the elephants have created in Tsavo East in the last few years a new phenomenon caused by falsely confining them to a small (for elephants) area? Have they really never before knocked down and eaten baobab trees or is it just that they have not done it recently? Questions like these cannot be answered quickly and we can only hope the elephants still have enough space to survive whilst we find out. Perhaps the biggest problem is a psychological one for it is not easy to begin a research project knowing that it cannot be completed in one's own lifetime. Maybe we need to conceive of a series of studies that will not be completed for a thousand years. That would still only give us fifty generations of elephants. Fifty generations of mice could be studied in five years; no wonder we know more about mice than about elephants.

At present the pressures on elephant and other animals are increasing. Poaching for ivory has become rife so that in areas where it was easy to see elephant without really trying only a few years ago it is today difficult or impossible. New and hardier strains of maize now make it feasible to grow crops in areas where only five years ago there was virtually no human population. The Masai, who until now have grazed their cattle alongside the plains game, are beginning to plough their lands for wheat and corn. Other threats are posed by the increased use of insecticides; the clearing of forests; the expansion of cities and towns; and, most frightening of all, the increase in the human population. At the turn of the century about 3 million people lived in Kenya. There are now 12 million, half of whom are under fifteen years old.

The men who started Kenya's wildlife sanctuaries were and are men of vision. They have worked against heavy odds often with inadequate resources. What is now needed is a sense of vision in Society as a whole—not Kenyan society but World society. Surely if the Egyptians could preserve a few corpses for 5,000 years we can manage the same with wild animals. It needs a sense of values which accepts that man is a lesser part of a greater whole—an unfashionable idea in our rushing, modern world, but one that becomes an obvious truth to any perceptive person who visits the remnants of Africa's glory. We now need a combination of measures designed to preserve wildlife for

A female ostrich.

A female ostrich.

A female Red-Backed Shrike, one of the many millions of migrant birds who winter every year in Africa. Netting studies have shown that birds weighing as little as 40 grams have made the Europe—Africa journey several times, returning to the same small area in Africa each winter.

Somali Ostrich race across the Chalbi Desert in northern Kenya.

centuries not decades, conceived and administered at international level.

Above all the pace at which we disturb the natural environment must be slowed down. Our startling success with the physical sciences has convinced us that we can now solve all our problems quickly by pressing the right buttons. But in nature problems are not solved quickly, although they can be created overnight. A disturbance of the established order is a wound, quickly inflicted but slow to heal, with the ever-present possibility that the wound may cause a fatal infection. Even a carefully thought-out and well-controlled change is still a form of surgery from which the environment must recover by adjusting its complex mechanisms and balances to the new situation. Since life began the environment has been adjusting itself to all manner of changes; today it is the speed of change which is new and potentially disastrous.

A century ago man himself was part of the established order. The elephant hunters had been around for so long that they did not threaten the survival of the elephant any more than lions threaten the survival of the plains game. The men of the Liangulu tribe—great elephant hunters who used bows stronger than the English long bow—had a toughness and knowledge which gave their way of life its own nobility, in strong contrast to the furtive moral squalor of the international racketeers involved in today's ivory trade. Now, we humans are biologically out of control all over the world; and in the same sense that a city child must visit a farm to find that milk comes from cows, not bottles, so

Crowned Cranes are seen all over Kenya and can be made into pets; but although beautiful they never become house trained.

Masai Ostrich in a mating dance. Ostrich are normally silent but in the breeding season the male has a booming, low-pitched call.

most of us need to visit Africa to find where mankind came from. Even here there is a danger of losing touch with the past.

Kenya's land area is 224,000 square miles so that even Tsavo (at 8,000 square miles the largest of the Parks) is a pocket handkerchief in comparison with the ecological whole which existed a century ago. Today the Parks and Reserves are last-ditch defences for Kenya's wildlife and we must salute the men who set them up and maintain them against so many destructive forces. The long-term outcome is far from certain, but meanwhile it is our privilege that enough remains for us to glimpse the original glory at first hand, paradoxically benefiting from the transport and facilities which threatening technology has brought to Africa.

The slender security of this privilege makes it doubly sad that many visitors bring their own pace with them and so do not get the best out of their contact with Kenya's wildlife. Too much dashing from one Game Park to another, and when inside the Park, from one animal to another, does not allow the visitor to attune himself. The use of a vehicle is only an advantage in that it can get one close to the animals without alarming them. If it imposes a 20th-century rhythm on your visit to an area which still beats with the slow, sure pulse of pre-history you have failed to make the best use of your privilege.

Try to stay longer with each group of animals. They will reward you in their time not yours remember *they* are making

the decisions. There is so much to see one is tempted to rush; More than one hundred species of mammals in Kenya, ninety-five in the Masai Mara Reserve alone, if we include the bats and rodents; more species of birds in the 44 square miles of Nairobi National Park than in the whole of the British Isles. But birds and animals are not postage stamps or locomotive numbers to be ticked off on a list. Each of them has an individual character and fits into its own place in a complex system.

It is an easy matter to find a lion, watch him snooze, and rush off to find a rhino. If you stay with the lion you might find out something about his world and through him the world of other animals. Why we like lions so much and how they have achieved such an important place in the mythology and art of the last 5,000 years is something of a mystery. Perhaps because with their clean-cut profiles, well-set eyes and neat rounded ears they yield themselves so easily to anthropomorphism. We envy their tawny skin, deep chests and well-muscled shoulders, not to mention their arrogant posing as the king of beasts. After an hour in front of a lion he may look at you once and then it will be such a fleeting glance it does not acknowledge your existence. Lions will eat and drink, sleep and urinate; the youngsters will fight and play; they will even make love; and all within a few yards of your car; but they will never by so much as a look or a gesture admit that you are there.

In one of Kenya's Game Reserves I once followed a group of lions for five days. They made no kill in that time and I was sorry to have to leave without seeing the ultimate drama; but I learnt a little about lions in those few days and more about Africa than the tourists who visited several different parks in the same period.

It is the same with all the other animals, large or small. Quiet, patient observation will give you the greater rewards. Those long, still moments when the engine is turned off and the real life of the animals is going on around you must soak into the depths of your consciousness; so that many years from now your inner self will still feel the deep, warm strength of Africa, setting the mind's nerves tingling with the memory of Nature's richest canvas, her greatest drama, her most harmonious symphony.

Kenya's Lake Turkana (formerly Rudolf) contains the largest concentration of crocodile left anywhere in the world, now protected in the Sibiloi National Park at the north-east shore of the lake. They occur throughout Kenya in suitable rivers and lakes and have a varied diet; those of Lake Turkana eat mainly fish but elsewhere they will take any unwary animal (or human) they get the chance of.

Adult male buffaloes—usually regarded as the most dangerous animals in Africa—do not have much fear of lions. These young lions had not eaten for at least five days but the buffalo had no difficulty in warning them off, though no doubt it was a useful lesson on buffaloes. Had all the lions been full-grown and one buffalo been on its own then it could have been a different story.

These Dwarf Mongooses are the smallest of the six species of mongoose found in Kenya. They are delightful little animals with alert faces and quick, darting movements. Many Dwarf Mongooses make their homes in disused termite mounds like this pair. Pet mongooses are so fast they are a torment for any dog; they can nip and dart out of reach faster than a dog can snap at them.

Gerenuk are well adapted to reach up when browsing. They often feed standing on their hind legs to reach even higher than this. Living in arid and semi-desert country they have not been observed drinking. Presumably, like the Oryx and the camel, their body temperature rises in the day and falls at night to conserve evaporation loss.

There are many species of chameleon in Kenya. This is the Jackson's or Three Horned Chameleon. They have a remarkable range of colours—green, orange, yellow and red are all possible and they can even turn dark grey on a tarmac road. Colour changes, like their movements, are slow and they might take 10 minutes to cross a road with a strange, rhythmic to-and-fro rocking motion. Their independently swivelling eyes are disconcerting and although they are totally harmless many uneducated Kenyans fear to touch them, perhaps mentally classing them with snakes.

Grant's Gazelle grazing at dawn. Grant's are
widespread throughout Kenya and can still be
seen in large numbers outside the National Parks
and Reserves especially in ranching country.

Cheetah, as everybody knows, are the fastest animals on earth. Unfortunately they are on the decline because of their need for open country in which to hunt. Even in the National Parks and Reserves they have problems with hunts being disturbed by visitors who move vehicles in too close in their excitement to see everything. They need to eat more frequently than lion and are not powerful enough to protect their prey. One hastily gulped meal is the most a Cheetah can expect from a kill before the hyena, jackal, vulture and even lion move in.

A family group of females and calves move across the plains of Amboseli. Kilimanjaro (at 19,340 feet the highest mountain in Africa) is more than a pleasing backdrop; Amboseli's underground springs come from the slopes of the mountain which in this picture is 25 miles away.

An old bull elephant peacefully asleep against a tree.

Irritated by the mischievous behaviour of a family of baboons this elephant warns them off with a characteristic threat display.

Elephants feeding in dry bush country.

Unlike most non-primates cow elephants carry their milk between their forelegs and can be uncannily reminiscent of the human female.

A female wild dog with her puppies in the Masai Mara. Expert hunters, wild dogs normally kill at least once a day; the adults regurgitate meat for the puppies.

A group of Grevy Zebra on ranching land north of
Mount Kenya.

A young lioness lifting the carcass of a topi.

The Masai Mara Game Reserve has an abundance of plains game unrivalled in Kenya and consequently supports a large lion population. Here a family drinks at a pool soon after dawn.

This alert and hungry lion is watching a lioness hunt zebra. Subsequently he lost his supper by revealing himself just before the lioness made her charge; the few seconds' warning was enough for the zebras to escape. To be successful a lioness needs to close on her quarry in the first 25 yards and only about one in five lion hunts result in a kill; the efficiency of the king of beasts need be no embarrassment to human monarchs although perhaps his ability to sleep for 18 hours a day might give them cause for envy. An adult lion will need about 40 kg of meat every four or five days, which is equivalent to 20 zebras a year.

An alert lioness on the look-out for prey.

Lions will do anything in public. When the female is on heat she will arouse the male at regular intervals every 40 minutes. This can continue for days and has been observed to last as much as 60 hours, with sometimes another male taking over when the first has had enough. Watching lions mate arouses a very strong feeling of observing a mechanism; something is happening to the lions without their making any decision about it. In spite of the large number of copulations the female does not always conceive.

1 Dawn over the Indian Ocean from the south coast of Kenya

2 Basket sellers on Diani beach, 20 miles south of Mombasa

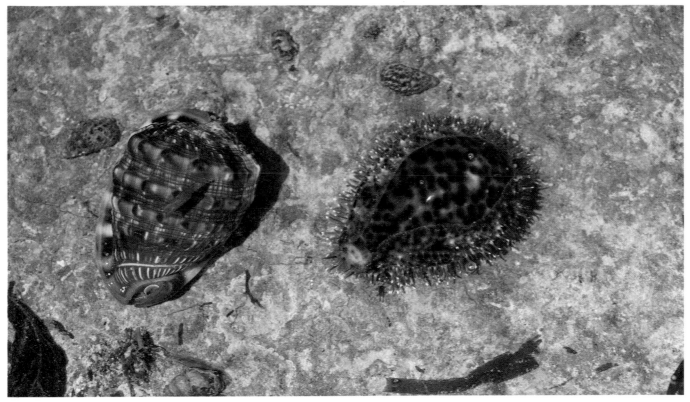

Left:

3 A typical Sambuk dhow from the Persian Gulf moored in Mombasa's old harbour

4 A Helmet shell (Cypraeicassis Rufa) and a Tiger Cowrie (Cypraea Tigris). Note the mantle on the cowrie which can retract or extend completely to cover and camouflage the shell

5 This colourful basket was the morning's catch of a Giriama fisherman taken from the coral reef 25 miles north of Mombasa. There are over 2,000 species of fish to be seen on Kenya's coral coast

6 Two dugout sailing canoes on Kenya's south coast

Below:

7 Beached sailing canoes on Diani beach

Right:

8 Elephant and Kilimanjaro in Amboseli

9 Common Zebra and White Bearded Gnu grazing in the Masai Mara Game Reserve in southern Kenya

10 Two lionesses and gnu in
Amboseli

11 African Scops Owl. This tiny 7″ owl is fond of the bush, savannah and woodland areas of Kenya's Parks and Reserves

12 Baobab tree at sunset

Above left:

13 Bateleur Eagles are common in Kenya and are frequently seen in game country

Above:

14 There are at least 25 species of starling recorded in Kenya, most of them gorgeous flying jewels. This one, the Superb Starling, is one of the commonest: all visitors enjoy him for he is found throughout Kenya and has little fear of man. In some lodges he may even join your table

15 Agama Lizards, common in hot dry areas, are often seen close to lodges

16 A group of Masai nomads
   on the move. It is no
   coincidence that Kenya's
   best-stocked Parks and
   Reserves adjoin Masai land.
   Traditionally the Masai tolerate
   wild animals and do not poach or
   hunt them

17 Lion with thorns

A lioness with cubs in the Masai Mara Game Reserve.

These are Olive Baboons, the larger and more common of Kenya's two species. They are absorbing animals to watch as they have a close knit family life. Female baboons will sometimes compete for the privilege of holding an infant which is not their own. Adult males are strong and dangerous being much more than a match for an Alsatian dog. They have a very varied diet, eating fruit, berries, insects, small gazelle, eggs, young birds—just like men in fact. In rural areas they often trouble farmers by raiding crops and have been known to throw stones at villagers who have to join in bands to drive them off.

Black-Faced Vervet Monkeys are pretty creatures often seen around Lodges throughout Kenya, where they are not above stealing food off the tables. Quite a number live in gardens in the suburbs of Nairobi but their real habitat is acacia woodlands not too far from water where they often live in large troops.

In spite of all adaptations every animal is defeated sometimes. This gnu has succumbed on the dried-out lake-bed near Amboseli during a severe drought.

Although hippos do not win any prizes for beauty out of the water, they do move with surprising grace underneath, when with ears and nostrils closed they take huge, slow-motion strides. In Tsavo West National Park there is an underwater observation tank at Mzima Springs where visitors will always see hippo and with luck can watch one walk past below the surface. Hippos are fairly common in suitable waters throughout Kenya and can even be seen inside the town boundary at Kisumu on Lake Victoria. One of the best places to see them out of the water is on the Mara River in the Masai Mara Game Reserve where on a cool morning they will sometimes stay out of the water for several hours. Not everyone knows that the hippo's diet is mainly grass and that they often travel several miles from water whilst grazing at night. They must wallow on sunny days or they overheat.

The Sable Antelope is only found in Kenya in the
Shimba Hills National Reserve, a few miles from
the coast, south of Mombasa; they are more
common further south in Africa. Amongst the
most handsome of the antelopes they have
inflicted fatal injuries on the belly of more than
one lion.

Left:
This young man is a Masai Moran. He has been initiated but is not yet married. Before marriage his hair will be shaved and he will become an elder.

Right:
Throughout Kenya, in the vast majority of tribal groups, the tradition is that only the young unmarried men will wear their hair long. Everyone else—including young women like this one—shave their heads, although the fairer sex find plenty of other ways of adorning themselves. It is no coincidence that so many of Kenya's National Parks and Game Reserves are in Masai land or have Masai people living on their boundaries. The Masai are traditionally tolerant of wild-life and will not normally eat game meat, preferring the milk of their own cows. It is the custom for a young man to spear a lion to death to prove his valour but apart from this they have not interfered with wild animals. Even today it is common to see Masai grazing their cows alongside zebra, gnu, gazelle and giraffe.

These are Grevy's Zebra which
occur only in the northern part of
Kenya; they are heavier and taller
than the Common Zebra found
further south. With their narrow
stripes and large fringed ears they
are also more handsome and the
skins more valuable.
Consequently they have been
heavily poached and are now
more difficult to see than they
were even a few years ago. They
can survive in very dry country
and so can be seen in the new
Sibiloi National Park on the
north-east shores of Lake Turkana.

To many the wildebeest, or White-Bearded Gnu, is an amusing animal; it has been said that he seems a creature designed by a committee. It must, however, be an efficient design for the gnu is the most prolific of the larger animals. There are around 3 million in Kenya and Tanzania where many of them take part in the famous Serengeti migrations. The Masai Mara Game Reserve (which adjoins the Serengeti) can contain unbelievable numbers of gnu when the migrations pass through. In this picture a herd is moving to water over the short and fragile saline grasses of Amboseli's dried-out lake-bed.

A group of Masai Giraffe.

Left:
These two male Masai Giraffe are necking, a
seemingly homosexual activity. The two males
may continue rubbing and striking their necks
together for as much as 30 minutes, occasionally
swinging their heads with great violence. Most
observers interpret the performance as a trial of
strength between rivals.

A rhino in Amboseli at the foot of
Kilimanjaro.

Black Rhinoceros are not always as docile as this; when alarmed they are unpredictable and very agile. Weighing up to $2\frac{1}{2}$ tons they are best treated with respect. Much poached for their horns (believed in Asia to be aphrodisiac—perhaps because rhino take over half an hour to mate) they have been exterminated in large areas of Kenya. Black rhinos are browsers, eating bushes, and many have been lost in Tsavo East National Park through drought; like elephants they die of starvation, not thirst, when there is no new growth. A big campaign to save rhino was launched in 1979; fortunately it is still possible to see them in most of the larger Parks and Reserves.

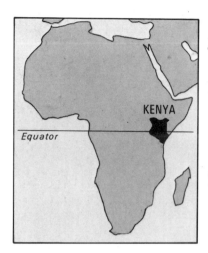

SUDAN

ETHIOPIA

UGANDA

SOMALI REPUBLIC

Lake
Turkana
(Rudolf)

Lodwar •

• Moyale

• Marsabit

• Wajir

▲ Mt Elgon
14178 ft

Lake Baringo

Eldoret •

Lake
Bogoria
(Hannington)

• Isiolo

Nanyuki

• Kisumu

Nakuru

▲ Mount Kenya 17058 ft

Equator

L. Nakuru

L. Elmenteita

• Garissa

L. Naivasha

Lake
Victoria

⊙ NAIROBI

Lake
Magadi

TANZANIA

Kilimanjaro ▲
19340 ft

Lake
Jipe

• Malindi

INDIAN

• Mombasa

OCEAN

0   100
                    miles
                    km
         150

KENYA

Equator

3 The Lakes

Kenya is rich in inland waters which vary from frozen mountain tarns to steaming, alkaline lakes fed by hot springs.

Lake Victoria, Africa's largest and the world's second fresh water lake, was the target of early European travellers and is now an important feature of western Kenya. The total area of approximately 26,000 square miles is shared with Tanzania and Uganda, Kenya having the smallest share of 1,500 square miles. This still gives Kenya over 250 miles of lakeside around the Kavirondo Gulf—or, to use its true Luo name, the Winam Gulf. Twenty miles wide and sixty long the Gulf is backed by hills rising almost 4,000 feet above the lake, which although neglected by tourists is always picturesque and often beautiful. The lake itself is 3,700 feet above sea level and is surrounded by fertile country watered by rains created by the lake itself. Thousands of fishing villages line the shores and there are numerous islands, some inhabited like Rusinga Island where important fossils have been found.

The rest of Kenya's larger lakes are in the Rift Valley and most of them are alkaline. Lake Turkana, in the north, is the largest alkaline lake in the world, being 160 miles long. At a height of only 1,200 feet Lake Turkana is in a hot and arid region, being fed by the Omo river from the Ethiopian Highlands.

Until recently known as Lake Rudolf, this huge inland sea supports the world's largest concentration of crocodile, now protected in the Sibiloi National Park on its north-east shores. The crocodile here feed mainly on fish; tilapia and Nile perch are abundant, the perch growing to over 200 pounds. The bird life is very rich and islands in the lake are used by European migrant birds as well as providing a nesting site for Lesser Flamingoes.

Further south, other alkaline lakes are Bogoria, Nakuru, Elmenteita and Magadi. All these support large bird populations dependent on the blue-green algae which thrive in hot, alkaline waters. Millions of Lesser Flamingoes feed on the algae directly whilst many other species eat the fish which eat the algae. Birdlife is always spectacular at any of the Rift Valley lakes and when there are concentrations, as occur from time to time, the numbers are unbelievable.

Lake Nakaru is the first National Park in Africa to have been established for the sake of its avifauna; over one million Lesser Flamingoes have been known here. Sometimes there are tens of thousands of Great White Pelicans.

Lake Magadi, the most southerly of Kenya's Rift Valley lakes, is the world's second largest deposit of sodium carbonate. Again low down (1,900 feet) and hot, this lake is nevertheless beautiful and has its own wealth of bird-life.

North of Lake Nakuru is Lake Bogoria (formerly Lake Hannington). Nestling under a 2,000-foot escarpment, this is perhaps the most beautiful of Kenya's lakes. Fed by hot springs and geysers, it is sometimes thronged with flamingoes. Further north again is Lake Baringo, a fresh water lake, which has the largest nesting colony of Goliath Herons in East Africa. Unfortunately the area around the lake is spoiled by local erosion caused by overgrazing.

The other fresh water lake of the Rift Valley is Naivasha, attractive and popular with local people from Nairobi. It is the highest—and coolest—of the Rift Valley lakes for the floor of the Rift rises in an arch with Naivasha at its centre. Here there are lakeside hotels with boats for hire, fishing is popular and over 400 species of birds have been recorded.

At the foot of Kilimanjaro, on the border with Tanzania, Lake Jipe is lonely and beautiful. Big enough to be famous in England but almost unknown in Kenya, it is once again very rich in bird life. Not far from here is Lake Chala, a crystal-clear crater lake in a parasitic cone of Kilimanjaro, a forest of euphorbias on its steep banks.

There is another crater lake at Simbi a few miles from Lake Victoria in the South Nyanza Province of western Kenya, caused by a gas eruption. This crater contains alkaline water and is sometimes visited by large numbers of flamingoes.

Mount Marsabit, in northern Kenya, is a range of volcanic hills and also has its crater lakes. The best known is Lake Paradise, a favourite watering place for the large elephant which live in the mountain's forest.

Mount Kenya too has its lakes but these are caused by glacial erosion and are liberally sprinkled over the flanks of the mountain above the 12,000-foot contour. The largest of these is less than half a mile long but they have a beauty out of proportion to their size, nestling under the snow-capped peaks. The Curling Pond, just below Point Lenana, is permanently frozen over although it is only $10\frac{1}{2}$ miles from the equator.

Finally there are the seasonal lakes like Amboseli near Kilimanjaro. Normally an arid bowl of dust, Amboseli floods in the rains and acquires a limpid beauty in soft contrast to its more usual shimmering mirages.

Succouring men, birds and beasts, the lakes of Kenya are an important feature of the landscape. In the heat of Africa the eye is grateful for a sheet of water; the lakes, like jewels, stud the land.

A FEW YARDS inside the southern hemisphere the house faced south, its back to the equator.

From here the land dropped to the lake, a long ribbon of silver backed by hills. The lake was there always, but the hills came and went with the atmosphere.

In the rains, when the air was washed clean, the mountains marched along the southern edge of the Gulf towards the great, open lake. The far mountains were fifty miles away and in the vivid blue mornings the great distance pulled the eyes and gave a sense of freedom.

Mornings were always vivid; dew on the grass, warm sun, and the view of the lake insisting that you leave the house for the real world outside.

Rain came in the afternoons, operatic, exuberant and overwhelming. The first cloud would be small, almost insignificant, casting a brief, drifting shadow. An hour later the sky boiled upwards. Suddenly leaves would begin rustling as the first warnings stirred the air. Then, half a mile away, the trees would duck and sway on the hillside and people would begin running. You could hear the rain rushing towards you like a train, arriving with all the suddenness of an express going through a station; one moment a distant warning, the next an all-powerful presence, the water hurling itself out of the sky, a deafening clamour on the roof, the house suddenly an island in the rushing water. Standing at the windows we would thrill to the elemental power and brace ourselves for the flashing cannons of thunder which would mercilessly annihilate great trees, turning them to blackened stumps, in spite of the rushing rain. Sometimes there would be hailstones and an hour later in the evening sunshine the children would play excitedly with the strange white banks of hail in the tropical garden, whilst our cook would worry about his small patch of maize.

Later, towards midnight, with the lights out, we would open the curtains and listen to the shrilling cicadas and the little gecko lizards chasing the moths across the mosquito netting. Far to the south the storm would still be flickering, silently lighting the distant mountains which would leap out of the night with incredible clarity.

These storms are part of the power of the lake, which dominates the land around it, as the ocean dominates a coast. It is a fertile region, succoured by the good rainfall from the lake's moisture, and is densely populated—one of the most densely populated rural areas in Africa. Little clusters of homesteads sprinkle the countryside, wisps of smoke rising from the thatched roofs. Everywhere there are people, always a smile and a greeting.

Here we lived for five years, under the spell of the lake, whilst I taught at a Secondary School. Many of my pupils came from its shores and we were often invited to visit their homes.

On one occasion we visited a home near the mouth of the Kavirondo Gulf, about a mile from the lake shore. The home was a cluster of round thatched huts, small ones for storing food, larger ones for living and cooking.

On arrival we were enveloped in hospitality; all hands were shaken as we stepped into the compound and again as we entered

A Luo elder in traditional head-dress of hippo tusks and ostrich feathers. The Luo people live in western Kenya on the shores of Lake Victoria.

the thatched hut, for one must be welcomed to the house as well as to the land. Hands are not released after shaking but are held for a long moment; here there is time to savour the feeling of contact given by holding another man's hand. Inside there was tea with bread and margarine. Some of the cups and saucers had been bought specially for the occasion, filling us with guilt. We sat on wooden chairs in a circle. Slow, courteous talk revolved around the table, our host acting as interpreter. Outside, the sun was hot and brilliant but in the hut we were in cool shade, the light and air entering only by the gap under the eaves. Tea over, a walk was suggested. We went as far as the lake at a strolling pace using footpaths through other homesteads. The nearest tarmac road was fifty miles away and even the dirt road had finished a mile or so from our friend's home; our car was the first to reach his compound. As we strolled to the lake conversations began with neighbours fifty yards before we arrived and continued fifty yards after we had left, the words carrying in the still, hot air.

At the lake shore a boat is called for; our host had previously arranged this and the boatmen are his cousins. We each wait for the boat in our own manner; we are impatient, our host relaxed. He knows the boat will come so what purpose will impatience serve? The time slides past and the boat arrives. We all get in and the paddlers take us to a small island. It is uninhabited and the paddlers tell us it is full of snakes. They fear the snakes but we see nothing.

On the other side of the island they are fishing. A huge net with floats has been laid out in a crescent from a boat. The net is two hundred yards long and now the two ends are being pulled in. Three or four men tug rhythmically at each end of the rope; a chanting song keeps them together. Other men and youths sit in the shade and watch. Occasionally a man leaves the net and is replaced. The net comes in slowly and only we ourselves are anxious to see what is caught. As the crescent of the net shrinks to a small circle a ring of men swim to the floats. Still there is no haste; the gleaming net is gathered in and perhaps two pounds of minnows flash and jerk in the sun. This apparent failure excites little comment or interest; if they are hungry today the flow of time will carry them to tomorrow or the next day when perhaps the net will be filled.

Only 112 years ago this lake was the last great geographical problem of the world—according to Sir Roderick Murchison, then President of the Royal Geographical Society, 'the problem of all ages'.

The legendary lakes of East and Central Africa, said to be the source of the Nile, were first indicated by Erastothenes at the end of the 3rd century B.C., but they remained mere legends until John Hanning Speke became the first European to sight Lake Victoria on 3 August 1858.

Looking south across the Kavirondo or Winam Gulf of Lake Victoria from the Bunyore Hills. The equator crosses the land in the foreground.

'The view was one which, even in a well-known and explored country, would have arrested the traveller by its peaceful beauty. The islands, each swelling in a gentle slope to a rounded summit, clothed with wood between the rugged angular closely cropping rocks of granite, seemed mirrored in the calm surface of the lake; on which I here and there detected a small black speck, the tiny canoe of some Muanza fishcrman. On the gently shelving plain below me blue smoke curled above the trees, which here and there partially concealed villages and hamlets, their brown thatched roofs contrasting with the emerald green of the beautiful milk-bush . . .

'This is a far more extensive lake than Tanganyika; "so broad you could not see across it, and so long that nobody knew its length." '

For his achievement in reaching the lake the French Geographical Society awarded Speke their Gold Medal and the Royal Geographical Society gave him their Founder's Medal.

But this was far from the end of the problem, for Speke had only visited the southern end of the lake. Real proof of the source of the Nile could only be obtained at the northern end and so in 1860 Speke set out again, this time with Grant.

After two years' travelling, in which they marched around the south and west of the lake, they finally discovered the source of the Nile at Rippon Falls on 28 July 1862.

From here Speke followed the Nile downstream to reach Gondokoro (now Juba) six and a half months later. Unfortunately he had to leave the river and travel across country for part of this journey so that his proof of the Nile's source was not absolute. It fell to Baker, whom Speke met at Gondokoro, to travel upstream and finally clinch the matter in 1865.

After meeting Baker, Speke continued down the Nile, via Khartoum, before leaving for England, and so became the first man in history to cover the 2,300 miles of Africa which are drained by this, the greatest and most famous of all rivers. He had a hero's welcome in England—a public reception at Southampton and a special meeting of the Royal Geographic Society in his honour.

Today the sailing canoes which Speke described still fish the lake from hundreds of villages around its shores. An early start catches the breeze which carries the boats away from the land; later, as the day heats up, the convection wind veers round and brings them home at mid-day or early afternoon.

Once, a friend and I arranged to meet a fisherman and go out with him to his fishing ground. We left the Yacht Club, with its catamarans and Fireballs, in a borrowed motor boat and sailed two miles round the point into Africa.

Huddled in the bottom of the boat, hugging ourselves against the pre-dawn cold, we watched the Southern Cross in the upside-down tropical sky and searched the East for a gleam of sunrise. The black water rushed past as our outboard chugged along the shore of the lake round into the dark bay, where already the Luo fishermen were at their boats. The first sails floated past, silent as

Fishing boats at the village of Dunga, near Kisumu, with Homa mountain in the background.

Left:
This young Nandi woman is wearing the traditional dress for the *Ngetundet* or 'Coming Forth' ceremony. This follows a five-month period of initiation and marks the young woman's graduation as an adult, eligible for marriage.

Above:
These phallic symbols are used in the final stages of the *Ngetundet* when young Nandi girls become eligible for marriage.

owls, in sharp contrast to our two-stroke.

We followed Michael in our own boat when he sailed out, since I wanted pictures of him from a distance. Then, a mile from shore, he dropped his sail for a moment, we pulled alongside, climbed aboard and sent our own boat back to the village. As Michael gave the orders to his two boatmen and the sail rose and filled, the staccato sound of our engine dropped behind and the sweetness of temporarily leaving the machine age enveloped us.

Michael's boat is typical of the many Luo sailing canoes of Lake Victoria. Already in use when the first Europeans visited the lake, the Luo boats were the most advanced design of all the many lakeside tribes, although the Baganda were reputed to have a higher standard of workmanship.

A hundred years ago, when Stanley visited the lake, he found

the Baganda building canoes more than seventy feet long, with a beam of seven feet, carrying as many as sixty-four paddlers. The keels of these canoes were made out of a single hollowed-out tree trunk which formed the bottom of the boat. It was pointed at each end and had planks fastened on each side to give the canoe more freeboard. Alas, canoes of this size cannot be seen today but the modern Luo sailing canoe still has a solid piece of wood for the keel with planks fastened each side to form three wash-strakes. The keels have no depth and the canoes carry large sail areas, so managing them requires care and vigilance. There is no rudder and steering is done with a paddle held down into the water at the stern of the boat; this necessitates good muscles and stamina.

As we sailed several miles into the Gulf, Michael kept a close watch on his 'marks' on the surrounding hills for he had to find the end of his net, indicated only by a bamboo stake, sticking up three feet out of the water. To find this marker several miles off-shore is no mean feat and yet we came upon it with seeming ease and no to-and-fro searching.

Once the stake is found the sail comes down and the canoe is paddled along the length of the net. Here the lake is only about twelve feet deep and the net is weighted along one edge so that it lies on the bottom. The other edge has floats attached and the net thus stands on the bottom of the lake like a vertical fence. Michael's net is about one mile long and the full length must be pulled up, hand over hand. The hope is that there will be fish entangled in the mesh, caught by their gills as they swim and feed. In April, during the rains, there is a good chance of catching tilapia, a tasty fish with a relatively high cash value, but on our February morning the whole mile of net yielded only a catfish and three lungfish weighing perhaps three or four pounds each. I do not know which astonished me most; the fact of only catching four fish, after all this effort; or the equanimity with which Michael and his boatmen accepted it. But Michael knows he will have his good mornings and his bad ones, and told us there would be no big catches until the moon changed.

Patience is the virtue for this occupation. Half-way along the net the lake was choppy and hauling the net became difficult; so the paddling ceased, we drifted twenty yards, the small anchor was dropped and we waited for the turn of the wind. An hour later the lake was calm and the rest of the net was hauled up in a miniature doldrums.

After finishing work on the net we all lolled in the bottom of the boat in a lake of flat glass. The sun bored into us, stifling movement and conversation.

Then, slowly but inexorably, the air began to move towards the land and we inched back home under the big sail. For the first

Papyrus abounds on Lake Victoria, often breaking away from the shore to form huge, floating islands. Within living memory some Luo fishermen made rafts of papyrus; nowadays it is widely used for roofs and mats.

A typical Luo sailing canoe; skill and muscle are needed to overcome the lack of keel or rudder.

miles the boat moved with the wind, so that for us the air was breathless. But, almost imperceptibly, the wind rose until we were running at a good pace, enjoying the refreshing breeze.

As the wind increased we left other boats behind and were amongst the first back at the village after seven hours in the canoe. The other homecoming boats made a fine sight behind us, balancing their large, spreading, dhow-like sails.

Years ago the catches were much bigger and the tasty tilapia were common. The growing human population has put increasing pressure on the lake itself as well as on the land around it. But modern experts who have studied the fishing potential feel that the traditional methods probably benefit the greatest number of people. Any use of motorised boats would mean concentrating the limited rewards in the pockets of a smaller number of fishermen. And in any case the total reliability of the convection wind pattern makes nonsense of the economics of powered boats. The quiet and timeless beauty of the Luo sailing canoes will not be lost in this generation at least.

Water lilies on Lake Naivasha.

Lake Naivasha, popular with week-enders from Nairobi, is very rich in bird life.

In spite of the dense population the lakeside region retains many traditions. Apart from their boats the Luo people still use hand-made pots—often holding several gallons—and wooden stools carved in one piece from a solid trunk. Traditional thatched houses are a feature of the landscape, their mud floors finished with attractive patterns combed on to the floor whilst it is still wet. Food stores are built of intricate basket-work to form miniature round houses raised on stilts. In the nearby hills the Nandi people also keep many of their ancient ways alive. To these people their initiation ceremonies are still important milestones marking the transition between childhood and adult life. The Nandi have a proud history being one of the few tribes to have successfully challenged the Masai. When the railway was being built, in the first years of the century, the opposition of the

A Black-headed Heron and a Long-tailed Cormorant share the same nesting tree at Kisumu heronry, a few miles from Lake Victoria.

Nandi people held it up for some time almost within sight of Lake Victoria.

For the people of modern Kenya Lake Victoria is the most important of her inland waters both for the fish, the fresh water and the fertile land around it. Wildlife also exists in this largest of all African lakes; hippo and crocodile are still there and waterbirds are abundant. Indeed Kenya's most accessible and interesting heronry is just five miles from Kisumu, whilst hippo can even be seen inside the town boundary. But the soda lakes of the Rift Valley, although virtually useless to humans, have nowadays much greater concentrations of birds, so that relatively tiny Lake Nakuru is probably more famous in the modern world than Lake Victoria itself.

All the lakes of Kenya have been formed by volcanic activity

Lake Turkana is often known as the Jade Sea.
The green colour is caused by microscopic algae
which are the diet of the flamingoes.

or movements associated with it. The continuous evaporation of water from these lakes has made most of them alkaline so that Nakuru, Bogoria (formerly Lake Hannington) and Magadi are so rich in soda as to be dangerous to bathe in, never mind drink. Further north the much larger and deeper Lake Turkana (until recently Lake Rudolf) is also alkaline but can still be drunk without ill effects, although unpleasant to the taste.

Alkaline water, well-heated by the sun, can support a vigorous growth of blue-green algae which is the first stage in a food chain maintaining thousands, sometimes millions, of flamingoes and fish. The fish, in turn, feed pelicans, herons, cormorants and crocodiles. Thus each of Kenya's alkaline lakes is rich in wildlife.

These lakes are all in the Great Rift Valley and are dotted along a north–south line over 400 miles long. No two are the same and they are all worth visiting, each being beautiful in its own way. At times the bird life can be totally astonishing, although it must be remembered that birds are free to fly away! Most of the alkaline lakes fluctuate in level according to the local rainfall and this in turn affects the growth of algae on which the flamingoes feed. From time to time there are huge concentrations of lesser flamingoes; sometimes over a million on Lake Nakuru which is only five miles long.

Lake Nakuru was made into a National Park in 1960 and is the only Park in Africa established for its avifauna. Even when the numbers of flamingoes drop the bird life is still immensely rich with almost 400 species recorded. Enormous numbers of Great White Pelicans—sometimes tens of thousands—can be seen, although they are quite recent arrivals. In 1960 the alkaline-tolerant little fish Tilapia grahami was artificially introduced into the lake with the idea of controlling mosquito larvae. Not only was this successful but the fish multiplied to such an extent that they now support very large numbers of fish-eating birds of which the pelicans are the most spectacular.

Sixty miles further north, Lake Bogoria (formerly Lake Hannington) is scenically the most spectacular of Kenya's Rift Valley lakes being at the bottom of a 2,000-foot escarpment. Sometimes huge numbers of flamingoes congregate here, unbelievably beautiful as they fly across the lake in skeins of pink against the dark green background of the valley wall. The shores of Lake Bogoria abound in hot springs and geysers of relatively sweet water. The flamingoes come to drink at these springs where their waters mix with the more alkaline lake. In the early morning the cool air is filled with steam and the valley becomes a magic landscape of drifting mist and ethereal birds.

Although Lesser Flamingoes sometimes build their mud-cake nests at Lake Bogoria they do not seem to breed successfully there. The main breeding ground is in Tanzania on Lake Natron; but Greater Flamingoes breed in Kenya on Lake Elmenteita, a delightful little lake in a moonlike landscape of old volcanoes. Unfortunately for travellers, but fortunately for the flamingoes, the shores of Lake Elmenteita are private land and so to most people it is just a pretty view from the main Nairobi–Nakuru road.

In contrast, Lake Naivasha is Kenya's most exploited lake and is

A Yellow-billed Stork and an immature Sacred Ibis share a tree at Kisumu heronry.

Happy Turkana children at Ferguson's Gulf on the west side of Lake Turkana.

very well known. Here boats may be hired and there is a choice of lakeside hotels; but the lake is by no means spoiled and is once again very rich in bird life with around 400 species recorded. This lake is roughly circular and about ten miles in diameter; Mount Longonot rises to over 9,000 feet just eight miles from the lake shore adding drama to an already picturesque setting.

Lake Naivasha is unusual amongst the Rift Valley lakes being of fresh water even though there is no surface outlet stream. Presumably there is an underground drainage system which helps to keep the water sweet. Because of this, Lake Naivasha and its surroundings have changed radically during the last eighty years. Originally there was only one species of fish in the lake. Tilapia were introduced and multiplied to excess; so black bass were introduced to control the tilapia. This seems to have worked well for the fish attract a large variety of birds. There are about eighty pairs of fish eagles around the lake together with many other fish-eating birds.

Unfortunately two other introductions have been less successful. Salvinia—a water fern—is now a real nuisance along the shore line. And the coypus—an aquatic rodent which probably escaped from a fur farm—are also undesirable as they eat too much vegetation, rejecting only salvinia. As usual man's changes are at best a mixed blessing.

Being 6,181 feet above sea level, Naivasha enjoys a pleasant climate of warm, sunny days and cool nights. Eighty miles due south, Lake Magadi is down at 1,900 feet—a low altitude in East Africa—and is in semi-desert country. Here the hot, dry air has been evaporating for millennia and has created the second largest deposit of sodium carbonates, or trona, in the world. This is the basis of an important industry but Lake Magadi is eighteen miles long and only the central section is disfigured by the factory and its pipe-lines. The southern end is still unspoiled and usually alive with flamingoes and other water birds. Around the lake many hills rise abruptly, the Nguruman Escarpment reaching 7,500 feet to the west. The trona of the lake itself is fascinating, covering huge areas of the dried-out lake-bed with pink crystals. From a distance the rose-pink lake shimmers on the valley floor surrounded by blue-grey hills. Hot springs around the shore add to this tropical extravaganza.

Many of Kenya's lakes were key points to the early European visitors. Tiny Lake Jipe at the foot of Kilimanjaro and now in the corner of Tsavo West National Park was one such place, highly praised by early travellers like Thomson, Rebmann and Krapf who found good supplies of food there. Lake Baringo was another staging post, famous eighty years ago for its lush plenty, now alas spoiled by overgrazing. Even today, Kenya's major road and railway skirt in turn Lake Naivasha, Elmenteita and Nakuru, repeating the route of many early travellers.

Only Lake Rudolf, or Turkana as it is now called, disappointed its first European visitors. Paradoxically this lake is perhaps the most rewarding of all to a modern visitor who is willing to accept minor discomfort. The largest alkaline lake in the world, Lake Turkana is over 150 miles long and up to thirty wide. Surrounded by rugged desert country it is a striking

Lake Magadi is the most alkaline of Kenya's Rift
Valley lakes; here evaporation has concentrated
the soda to create the second largest deposit in
the world.

An African Spoonbill feeding its young with fish caught in Lake Victoria. Several fish are stored inside the gullet and the young birds must tug vigorously to get them out.

introduction to a remote area, where the very deserts which tried the early Europeans add to the modern traveller's feeling of adventure.

Very rich in fish, Lake Turkana is one of the few places in the world where even a novice can guarantee to catch something. Nile perch grow up to 200 pounds in weight and support a fishing industry on the western shore. Once again the plentiful fish support a very large and varied bird population. Pelicans are common and so are flamingoes which feed on the blue-green algae that grow in the alkaline water and give the lake its popular name, the Jade Sea. Crocodiles abound and feed almost exclusively on fish—although there have been fatal accidents, so nothing should be taken for granted. The largest remaining crocodile population in the world is now protected in the Sibiloi National Park on the north-east shores of the lake. There are in the region of 13,000 crocodiles here and since the alkaline water gives them a growth called 'buttons' they should be safe for many years. The growth makes the skins useless to the leather trade.

At one time Lake Turkana was 600 feet deeper than it is today and used to flow into the Nile, which accounts for the presence of the Nile perch. As the lake has gradually dried out a very rich fossil record has been left on its old shores and it is here that important finds, throwing light on man's origins, have recently been made. At Koobi Fora, roughly in the centre of Sibiloi National Park, a skull estimated to be 2,800,000 years old was found in 1969 and since then excavations have continued to yield further discoveries.

A century ago, when Speke finally reached Lake Victoria and solved the great geographical problem of the source of the Nile, Kenya was truly an explorer's country. Today, in spite of all the changes, we can still indulge something of the feeling of adventure that the early traveller's stories arouse by making our own journey through the northern deserts to the hot and stormy inland sea which received its first European visitors less than a hundred years ago.

This journey is described in Chapter 5.

Overleaf:
Lesser Flamingoes on Lake Magadi.

An El Molo man crossing crocodile-infested waters from El Molo Island to the east shore of Lake Turkana. His raft is made from doum palms.

The Saddle-bill Stork is the most handsome of all
the storks. Although rare in Kenya, a few pairs
breed in Amboseli.

A Luo boy with a new-born goat kid. Although
the Luo grow varied crops and many of them fish,
livestock is their main interest.

Lake Bogoria is the most spectacular
of Kenya's Rift Valley Lakes. The valley scarp
drops 2,700 feet to the lake shore where hot
springs and geysers abound.

A Yellow-billed Stork landing at Kisumu heronry.

Right:
Sunset on Lake Jipe, Tsavo West
National Park.

Lesser Flamingoes on Lake Turkana.

A Turkana woman with her camels at Lake
Turkana.

A Turkana girl on the sandy shore of Lake Turkana.

A Goliath Heron at Lake
Naivasha. The largest of the
Herons, they can be up to 5 feet
tall.

Lake Jipe is on the border of Tanzania, close to
Kilimanjaro.

Black-headed Heron and young
at Kisumu heronry.

Overleaf:
Pelicans, flamingoes, spoonbills
and cormorants on Lake Nakuru.

A Pink-backed Pelican on Lake Naivasha.

The African Fish Eagle has a characteristic gull-
like cry, evocative of wild places.

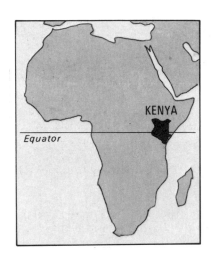

KENYA

Equator

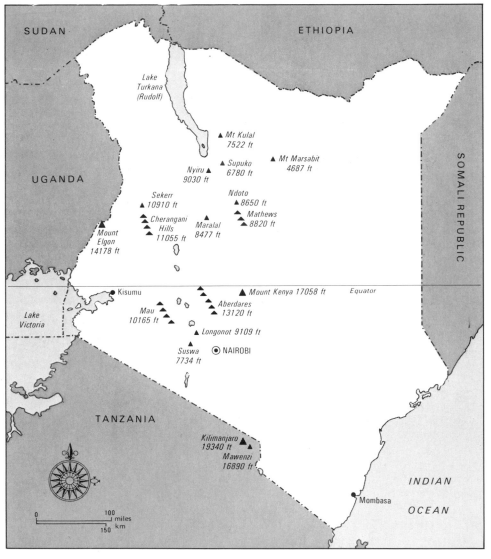

SUDAN

ETHIOPIA

*Lake
Turkana
(Rudolf)*

▲ *Mt Kulal
7522 ft*

UGANDA

Nyiru ▲
9030 ft

▲ *Supuko
6780 ft*

▲ *Mt Marsabit
4687 ft*

SOMALI REPUBLIC

*Sekerr
10910 ft* ▲

Ndoto
▲ *8650 ft*

*Cherangani
Hills
11055 ft* ▲

*Maralal
8477 ft* ▲

▲ *Mathews
8820 ft*

*Mount
Elgon
14178 ft* ▲

● Kisumu

▲ *Mount Kenya 17058 ft*

Equator

*Lake
Victoria*

*Mau
10165 ft* ▲

*Aberdares
13120 ft*

▲ *Longonot 9109 ft*

*Suswa
7734 ft* ▲

◉ NAIROBI

TANZANIA

*Kilimanjaro
19340 ft* ▲

*Mawenzi
16890 ft*

INDIAN

● Mombasa

OCEAN

100
└─┴─┴─┴─┴─┘ miles
0   ┬
        150 km

138

4 The Mountains

Almost all Kenya's mountains are volcanic in origin, formed through weaknesses in the earth's crust associated with the Rift Valley which splits Kenya from north to south on its way from the Red Sea to southern Africa.

Kilimanjaro, just south of the border between Kenya and Tanzania, is 19,340 feet high and is Africa's highest mountain. There are three peaks on the mountain mass of Kilimanjaro, Shira and Mawenzi being very much older than Kibo, the most recent and highest peak. The crater of Kibo is perfectly formed and clearly shows the history of the mountain which has had three major eruptions, collapsing each time, so that there is now a caldera, or outer crater, an inner crater and an Ash Pit which is over 400 feet deep. Fumaroles still spout steam and gases in the sides of the inner crater and the Ash Pit so the mountain is dormant, not extinct.

Like so many of East Africa's mountains, Kilimanjaro is isolated so that it can be seen from great distances. It is an important feature in southern Kenya's landscape and on clear days, especially after rain, can be awe-inspiring for it towers three and a half vertical miles above the surrounding plains. I have seen it several times from Nairobi, 130 miles away, and there are records of sightings from Mount Kenya which is a distance of 210 miles.

Mount Kenya is the second highest mountain in Africa and is more ancient than Kilimanjaro, being around one million years old. It is estimated that at one time it was higher than Kibo, having probably been as much as 23,000 feet. When Kilimanjaro ceased erupting the molten lava was withdrawn, allowing the peak to collapse and form a caldera; but in the case of Mount Kenya the lava remained inside the vent and cooled slowly to form hard, crystalline rocks. Over the millennia the surrounding ash has been eroded, leaving the central plug exposed as a jagged tooth rising 2,000 feet above the gentler slopes of ash and pumice. Hanging from this tooth of rock are 12 small glaciers, the longest being the Lewis glacier currently about 900 yards long. At the present time the glaciers are retreating on Mount Kenya (and Kilimanjaro), the Lewis glacier having lost over 200 yards in the last 40 years. If the present trend continues, the glaciers could have disappeared by the end of the century but a slight change in climate could prevent this. 150 years ago, the glaciers were more extensive. The mountain carries plenty of evidence of the true ice age for there are 32 glacially eroded tarns strewn around the mountain flanks.

Lower down, elephant and buffalo abound in the forest belt which circles the mountain, whilst above the 11,000-foot contour a profusion of plants unique to equatorial mountains decorate the moorlands. A chain of mountain huts aids access to the mountain which was made into a National Park in 1949. Non-mountaineers can have a very worthwhile trip to the mountain by climbing Point Lenana which, at 16,260 feet, is higher than Mont Blanc but requires no mountaineering skill.

Several other mountains in Kenya have National Parks. South-west of Mount Kenya the Aberdares reach over 13,000 feet to create a huge mass of high, rolling moorland alive with flowers and waterfalls. Lower down, forest and bamboo shelter a wealth of creatures including the rare and shy Bongo, numerous other antelopes, together with elephant, buffalo and rhino. Melanistic leopards and serval cats are more common at high altitude and the serval cats in particular are easy to observe on the Aberdares.

Mount Elgon on Kenya's western border is also high, reaching 14,178 feet, and again has a wealth of wildlife. The south-east slopes of the mountain have been declared a National Park where all the major mammals of the forest may be seen. Black and white Colobus monkeys are a feature here with splendid capes of fur streaming behind them as they leap from branch to branch.

Mount Elgon is a very old volcano with a large caldera containing a forest of Tree Groundsels. Hot springs still bubble out of the crater floor which is drained by the Suam river that runs through a spectacular gorge breaching the caldera wall. Lower down in the National Park, a number of huge caves harbour tens of thousands of bats.

Caves are a feature of many Kenyan mountains. Most of these are lava tubes left empty when molten lava ran out of the volcano under a surface of cooled and solidified rock. Mount Suswa in the Rift Valley has an extensive system of caves and the Chulu Hills, on the edge of Tsavo West National Park, has one of the biggest cave systems in the world, still not fully explored. Shitani at the southern end of the range is a very new volcano indeed, probably only two or three centuries old. It is easy to climb this peak and look down into the crater; at the foot of Shitani a lava tube cave has been opened up for visitors.

Over most of Kenya, volcanoes old and new rise out of the plains to delight the eye. Only the north-east towards Somalia is flat and dull. Elsewhere an hour's drive will always bring a range of hills to punctuate the horizon. This gives the landscape an enormous spaciousness, often range after range leading the eye to the infinite so that here one thinks in hundreds of miles rather than in scores. Apart from the coastal strip, most of Kenya is far above sea level, Nairobi itself being at 5,500 feet. It is a high land of high hills, filled with clear mountain air.

The south-east face of Mount
Kenya.

THOSE BROUGHT UP in a modern society must make an inner, personal journey if they are to meet the real and natural world on which our society ultimately depends. Like many Englishmen I began this journey tramping the hills of Cumberland where the clean wide spaces of the fells opened my mind to the even greater spaces beyond. Later I found myself spending half the year dreaming and planning for the few weeks of mountain holiday in Norway or Austria, France or Italy.

From the high summits of the Alps the cities of Europe seem irrelevant. In clear, blue, frozen mornings the great range notches its way into the infinite as it marches a thousand miles across the top of Italy. Here, in the pure air, the eye is pulled outwards and the furthest peaks draw the mind to other continents with yet more distant ranges.

Thus the chance to come and live in Kenya proved irresistible, with its promise of still higher peaks in a relatively empty continent. And on arrival the ascent of Mount Kenya became a personal priority, as though I would only get a proper perspective of the country from the summit of its highest peak.

Mount Kenya is not an easy mountain by European standards. Alpinists grade climbs on a scale of difficulty from 1 to 6 and the easiest route to the summit of Mount Kenya is grade 4. Most of the major peaks in Europe, including the Matterhorn and Mont Blanc, can be climbed by a route of lower grade than this; and of course at 17,058 feet Mount Kenya is considerably higher than any mountain in the Alps. From the mountaineer's viewpoint Mount Kenya is a splendid peak; Eric Shipton, who with P. Wyn Harris formed only the second party to reach the summit in 1929, has written:

'I know no mountain in the Alps, with the possible exception of Mont Blanc, that presents such a superb complexity of ridges and faces as the twin peaks of Mount Kenya—a complexity that would delight the heart of any mountaineer. Each feature is clear cut and definite, none is superfluous to the whole lovely structure. It would take many years of climbing holidays to explore them all, and each would involve a high standard of mountaineering.'

Today several different routes to the summit have been established, some of them of a very high standard indeed, requiring the use of the latest mountaineering aids and equipment.

I was lucky enough to make friends with an Austrian, who also had plenty of Alpine experience, so that once we were on the main mountain we both felt at home. But the approach to the central rock peaks could hardly be more different from the approach to an Alpine peak in modern Europe.

Mount Kenya is an old volcano with a large base; the lower slopes are a huge mound of lava sixty miles in diameter and overgrown with ancient forest and alpine moorland. Rising out of this enormous mound the central peaks are a jagged spike of crystalline rocks which originally blocked the throat of the volcano. The surrounding lava is relatively soft and has eroded

Left:
The author's bivouac site, just below the summit of Batian on Mount Kenya. At 17,058 ft this is the second highest point in Africa.

Tree Groundsels are a feature of East African mountains. These are near the summit of Mount Elgon at almost 14,000 ft.

more quickly than the central peaks so that today, perhaps a million years after the eruptions ceased, the central core is prominently exposed.

To climb the mountain you must first walk up the relatively gentle slopes of lava before tackling the steep, central peaks. On the first successful ascent in 1899 Halford Mackinder employed two Italian guides from Courmayeur at the foot of Mont Blanc. Accompanied by over 150 porters this party managed to hack its way through the forest in only one day—a considerable feat as anyone who has walked up the now well-established routes will testify. Today it is possible to drive to around 10,000 feet leaving only a few miles of forest track to be completed on foot. It is wise to stick carefully to the established paths for the forest is full of game including rhino, elephant and buffalo. There have been

Looking down from Uhuru Peak, 19,340 ft, the summit of Kilimanjaro and the highest point in Africa. The rock peak in the clouds is Mawenzi (16,890 ft), a much older mountain. Kilimanjaro still has fumaroles puffing steam in the crater. The glaciers on Kili are currently receding— hence the spectacular ice cliffs. Although inside Tanzania, Kilimanjaro adds much to the scenery of southern Kenya and can be seen from Nairobi, 130 miles away, on a clear day.

some unfortunate accidents to people who have unwittingly got mixed up with a herd of elephant when wandering off the main track but normally the big game will avoid contact with humans. The buffalo of Mount Kenya are, according to one authority, the largest in all Africa.

Flowers and butterflies are a feature of the forest and it is often possible to see Sykes or Colobus monkeys in the trees. Curiously the forest ends abruptly so that viewed from above it seems like an enormous hedge. Ascending, one is suddenly released from the confining trees on to the open moor with its wealth of strange plants peculiar to equatorial mountains. Here giant heaths and heathers up to fifteen feet tall dot the landscape to create a park-like scene. Lobelias grow lovely eight-foot spikes of blue-green flowers and Giant Groundsels grow to twenty feet on fragile, brittle stems. Vast numbers of smaller flowers grace the ground which in some places is carpeted with everlasting Helichrysums.

These giant plants are adapted to the rather special climate of equatorial mountains and they can be found above 10,000 feet all over East Africa. There is very little wind on the high peaks of this region and so many of the plants, though tall, are fragile. But they have problems other than wind to contend with at 13,000 feet where daily mists cut down the available sunlight and clear nights give hard frosts. The Giant Lobelia, for example, opens its leaves with the dark green shiny surface upwards in the day and closes them at night, presenting the furry and silver underside to the cold, dark sky.

For most days in the year the weather pattern is the same; dawns are clear and brilliant with the peaks towering in an empty sky. By mid-morning clouds are swirling round their feet and well before noon the peaks are enveloped in mists. Often these mists roll away an hour before sunset to reveal the peaks, perhaps with a new dusting of snow. To the mountaineer this weather pattern is frustrating; an average climber's day begins with a dawn of sparkling frost and the first hours of climbing will be blessed with sunshine. Then the mists will begin swirling round the peaks and well before the summit is reached it is difficult to see a rope's length ahead. Much later, on the descent, the clouds may roll apart and give a brief hour's sunshine in the evening; the climber, now far below, looks up to see the jagged peaks rising once more into a clear blue sky—taunting his memory of the misty summit he trod a few brief hours before.

Norbert, my Austrian friend, and I climbed Batian this way and shared the summit mists together at around two o'clock in the afternoon. Our descent was hampered by showers of snow and sleet so that by the time the clouds cleared at six in the evening we were still on the north face, far above the easy ground we had left that morning. We continued the descent, using torches to reach Kami Hut at 14,564 feet well after dark. Next morning, as we started to walk off the mountain, the peaks were once again soaring into a pure blue dome and we resolved to return and sleep on the very top of the mountain in the hope of beating the daily mists.

Mount Kenya from the Teleki Valley with Giant Groundsel and Lobelia in the foreground.

Left:
Early morning frost is common in Kenya's
mountain areas, even close to the equator.

'Old Man's Beard' decorates trees in mountain
forests all over Kenya, including isolated
mountains in the desert regions.

For our second climb we spent two days reaching Kami Hut from the road head on the Naro Moru route. We enjoyed our walk through the forest; and again up over the moorlands to Teleki Hut at 13,000 feet where my thermometer registered 26°F only ten miles from the equator. The following day we traversed round the mountain to Kami Hut through magnificent walking country, passing several delightful tarns on the way. The slopes of Mount Kenya are jewelled with thirty-two of these tarns, a feature which adds charm to an already splendid peak.

The following morning in the first grey light we were stumbling up the boulders above Kami Hut. Seven o'clock saw us roping up at the foot of the north face, in sparkling sunshine with hoar frost still lying in the shadows and cat-ice coating the mountain pools. Across the Mackinder Valley the peaks of Terere and Sendeo rose up to more than 15,000 feet and still looked high, but immediately above us were the 2,000-foot summit crags of Batian, Kenya's highest peak. The first few hundred feet of this route follow a natural gully where easy climbing soon brought us to a large amphitheatre up which we could scramble without a rope. From here we could enjoy fine views to the north, across the face of the mountain to snow-capped Point Lenana, which is the third highest peak of Mount Kenya and within the powers of any strong walker, without the need of ropes.

Above the amphitheatre we took it in turns to lead up a steep rock tower, hauling our heavy rucksacks up the harder parts. Then another short climb and a scramble brought us to the main West Ridge of the mountain. By this time we were surrounded by swirling mist with occasional glimpses of ridges dropping away from us to the glaciers 2,000 feet below. For a few moments we enjoyed a spectre of the Broken, an unusual atmospheric effect where the viewer sees his own magnified shadow on a cloud, surrounded by a coloured halo.

Now we continued along the ridge going mainly up and sometimes down until we reached Shipton's notch, a prominent gap in the ridge. We roped down into this and then continued up the last 200 feet.

Intending to sleep on the summit, we had not hurried the climb, and in answer to our hopes the clouds began to fret away as we arrived. The last hour of the day was what we had dreamed of; the mist swirled and broke, revealing first the closer pinnacles and ridges, then the Tyndall glacier far below, its surface reamed with crevasses. Shafts of sunbeams struck the West Ridge flooding its battlements with yellow light. Across the Gate of Mists (a narrow col which separates the twin peaks of Mount Kenya) Nelion stood out from a grey blanket. Within minutes the last shreds of mist dissolved and we found ourselves suddenly masters of the world, thrust upwards, thousands of feet above the surrounding land.

To the north and east, three vertical miles below us, the deserts of Kenya stretched away for ever, into the infinity of the coming night; whilst to the west the sun sank behind the distant Aberdares, whose 13,000 foot peaks cast fifty-mile-long shadows on to the vast, intervening plains.

For a brief moment we were isolated above the night-struck

Abseiling into Shipton's Notch on the West Ridge of Mount Kenya.

world, catching the sun's last threads of light on our pinnacle of gold; then the threads broke and rushed across the sky and we were back on cold, grey rock. A hand of frost touched our cheeks and we turned to the prosaic business of rucksacks, sleeping bags and gas stoves.

Fifteen feet below the summit we found a ledge eight feet long and five or six feet wide where we made ourselves as comfortable as possible for the night. Here in the thin air gas burns slowly and water boils at 180°F but we made soup and tea whilst lying in the cosy comfort of our sleeping bags.

Early in the morning the bivouac sheet brushed my face with frost and I pushed it aside to find the first light coming. Snuggling into the warmth of the bag and tugging against my belay rope I faced the dawn. A grey cloud-sea rolled away to the east; below me dark valleys hid beneath the light.

In fifteen minutes the sun made its sudden, equatorial entrance, painting the cloud-sea white and prising the secrets from the valleys. The hoar frost on the edge of my sleeping bag evaporated and three feet away my friend Norbert stirred. I sat up and began preparing tea. Whilst the stove hissed under a pan of snow we organised our gear and surveyed our kingdom.

A few hundred feet to the east was Nelion, Kenya's second highest point, and to the right the Hobley and Gorges valleys which lead down towards Embu. Beyond them at 12,000 feet, about a mile below us, the cloud-sea rolled away to the far distance, making its own horizon. To the north and west the distance was free of cloud, giving us views of the Northern Frontier District to Samburu and beyond. Around the slopes of the mountain the forest clung, skirt-like, the bamboo stands a paler green, seeming mown fields from this distance. Down there, three days ago, we had climbed the forest track and measured our footprints against the spoor of elephant and buffalo. Up here we were the only living things.

Immediately below us to the north-west was the ridge we had followed to the summit the day before. So narrow in places that one can sit astride it, '*à cheval*', this knife of rock gives breathless views of the glaciers 2,000 feet below. The Tyndall glacier, descending steeply with yawning crevasses up to thirty feet across, is reminiscent of the Alps, whilst the Lewis glacier descends more gently from Point Lenana and, being less steep, has few big crevasses. At this early hour it was in cold shadow but soon the full sun would be on it and only the daily mists around the summit prevent the glaciers from disappearing. Even this protection is not enough and all the glaciers are steadily receding. A small, but real, change in climate would be needed to save them. At the present rate they may disappear by the end of this century.

The tinkle of our pan lid brought us back to the reality of boiling water, brewing tea and the need for our descent. We abseiled down our doubled rope into the Gate of Mists and climbed to Nelion, using ice-axe and crampons up the steep snow, the flying chips of ice sparkling white against the deep blue sky.

On top of Nelion we barely had time to enjoy our new vantage point before the daily clouds stole up and enveloped us in a more

Hartlaub's Turaco in the forest of Mount Kenya.

Right:
The summit of Batian, Mt Kenya's highest point, taken from Nelion very early in the morning.

hostile world. We cast about on the summit, looking for our way, the icy gullies dropping into clinging vapours which hid the route. We chose a line and threw our double coil into space. The twin ropes vanished into greyness and we abseiled off into the swirling quiet of the mist. In August the south face can be full of snow and at one point, lower down, we abseiled through it, breaking the frozen crust and falling thigh deep into its creamy whiteness. The day became a routine of coiling, throwing, abseiling, pulling, coiling, throwing.

Crunching across the Lewis glacier in the first hour of darkness that evening, the frost already biting, it was strange to think we were less than ten miles from the Equator.

The next day, our tiredness leaving us, we walked down into the tropics, the greens deeper and more vivid for our two days on the summits. Down in the forest the occasional flowers blazed like flames and we kept alert for game. Buffalo-hooves had churned up the track ahead of us and in a steeper part a flurry of footprints and a broad slide mark showed where one had gone over in the slippery mud. The tracks looked fresh and, rounding a bend, we found an old bull facing us, thirty yards ahead. This was not like being in one's car on the plains of Amboseli. One stands near a tree and reflects on the relative objective dangers of walking at 9,000 feet and climbing at 17,000. After some minutes of mutual glaring he moved off into the forest—outfaced or bored—and we walked on in ostentatiously noisy conversation.

Half an hour later we were driving off the mountain, down through the forest and bamboo, back into tropical Africa.

Mount Kenya is the only mountain in the country which cannot be climbed without the use of real mountaineering techniques. Of course there are hundreds, probably thousands, of other peaks which have steep faces that would make splendid mountaineers' playgrounds, and on several cliffs keen climbers have already done many routes of a high standard. But by avoiding the more difficult faces it is possible just to walk up the rest of Kenya's mountains. Indeed even the highest peak in Africa, Kilimanjaro, which is just over the border in Tanzania, can be reached by a strong walker. But for those who enjoy mountain walking many of these other peaks are a delight.

In western Kenya, not far from Lake Victoria, Mount Elgon rises from a base seventy miles in diameter to a height of over 14,000 feet. This huge, ancient volcano has a greater wealth of tropical alpine plants than either Mount Kenya or Kilimanjaro. The floor of its caldera is a vast forest of Giant Groundsels and, although from a distance the mountain slopes seem gentle, once one is near the crater rim its great height becomes apparent and the mountain's isolation gives a sense of space not even to be found on the summits of the Alps.

This isolation is a feature of all Kenya's mountains so that even relatively minor peaks like Mount Suswa or Longonot have a grandeur out of proportion to their size. In northern Kenya there are hundreds of peaks which sprout out of the desert where a man who likes to use his legs could walk for months and never see a road. In Africa, as in Europe, the last refuges of peace will be in the hills.

The Great Rift Valley, which stretches from the Red Sea into southern Africa, caused a weakness in the Earth's crust through which all Kenya's volcanic mountains have erupted.

But for myself the real discovery has been to find that the thrill of Nature's wild and lonely beauty, which I first tasted in the solitude of high places, can also be found in the wide, open savannah, the dry bush country, the semi-desert plain. In Kenya it is not yet necessary to climb mountains to enjoy an untouched landscape.

In a way this increases the splendour of the peaks; uncrowded by cities, or the works of man, they remain aloof, timeless sentinels in a huge, eternal landscape. Sometimes, after rain, the high, thin air is so clear that peaks stand out a hundred miles away.

On such days this must be the most spacious land on earth.

This aerial view of Mount Kenya from the north-east shows (left to right) Point Lenana (16,355 ft), the Gregory Glacier and the twin peaks of Nelion (17,022 ft) and Batian (17,058 ft).

The Chania Falls, high in the Aberdares.

Sapuko (6,780 ft), 25 miles from the southern end of Lake Turkana, is typical of the hundreds of rocky peaks that erupt from the desert plains of northern Kenya.

Giant Groundsel at 14,000 ft on Mount Elgon in
western Kenya.

Elgon Tarn nestles just below the 14,140-ft peak
of Mount Elgon in a forest of Giant Groundsel.

18 Luo fisherman working a net on Lake Victoria

19 Lesser Flamingoes drinking at the hot springs of Lake Bogoria

20 Camels at Lake Turkana

21 Luo sailing canoe at dawn on Lake Victoria

22 Great White Pelicans, African Spoonbills and Lesser Flamingoes on Lake Nakuru

23 Yellow Billed Storks nesting at Kisumu heronry, near Lake Victoria

Left:

24 Batian and Nelion, the twin
peaks of Mount Kenya. Batian
(17,058 ft), behind and to the left
of Nelion, is slightly the higher of
the two

25 Looking down the West Ridge of
Mount Kenya from the very
summit of Batian in
the last rays of the evening sun

26 Descending Point Lenana
(16,355 ft). This subsidiary
peak of Mount Kenya is much
easier than the true summits but
is still higher than Mont Blanc -
the highest peak in Europe

Right:

27 A stream in the mountain
forest

28 Cotyledon Arbeyi on Mount Suswa

29 A male Mocker Swallowtail (Papilio dardanus) feeding on a Fire-ball Lily (Haemanthus Multiflorus); these lilies are common on many East African mountains. This one was on Marsabit Mountain in northern Kenya

30 Red-hot Pokers (Kniphofia) and fields of Everlastings (Helichrysum) at 10,000 ft in the Aberdares

31 Giant Lobelias grow between 12,000 and 15,000 ft on Mount Kenya

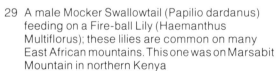

32 Samburu morans with their cows

33 Samburu moran dancing

34 A Rendille nomad encampment near Baragoi in northern Kenya

38 Beautiful Boran girls, northern Kenya

39 Gabbra people watering their camels in northern Kenya

Right:
The rocky peak of Sekerr rises to 10,910 ft at the northern end of the Cherangani Hills. Most of East Africa's mountains were formed by volcanic action; the Cheranganis are unusual, being the only fold mountains in Kenya.

Point Lenana (16,355 ft) is a subsidiary peak of Mt Kenya.

162

Mount Longonot (9,109 ft) is a familiar landmark seen from the Nairobi—Nakuru road. In this aerial view the mountain's volcanic origin is obvious; note the large patch of black lava on the flanks of the mountain, relic of a recent eruption.

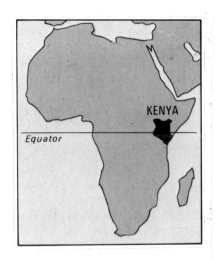

SUDAN

ETHIOPIA

KENYA

Equator

UGANDA

Lake
Turkana
(Rudolf)

Lodwar

El Molo

Turkana

Gabbra

CHALBI
DESERT

KOROLI
DESERT

Rendille

Boran

DIDA GALGALU
(Plain of Darkness)

Marsabit

SOMALI REPUBLIC

Mount Elgon

KAISUT
DESERT

Samburu

SABENA
DESERT

Kisumu

Mount Kenya

Equator

Lake
Victoria

⊙ NAIROBI

TANZANIA

Kilimanjaro ▲

INDIAN

OCEAN

Mombasa

Boran People

0   100
                          miles
                    150
                          km

Desert and semi desert
with less than 400mm of
rain per year

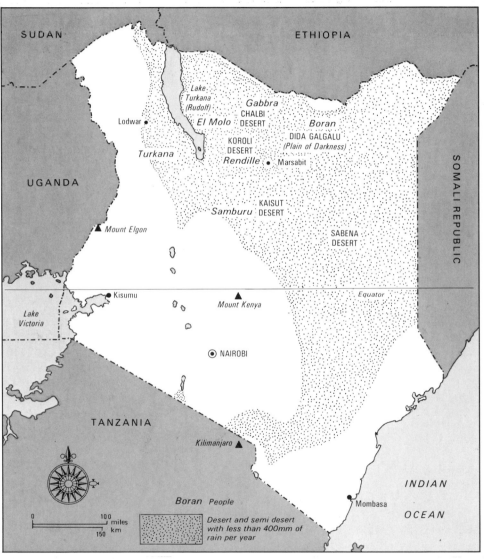

5 Desert Country

Almost half of Kenya's total land is semi-desert, receiving less than 15 inches of rain a year: in round figures 108,000 square miles, mainly to the north and east of the country whose total area is 224,000 square miles. The minimum rainfall needed for crops in Africa is 25 inches and so the entire population of the arid half of Kenya consists of nomadic pastoralists or hunter gatherers. The total population of this huge region (which is larger than Great Britain) is approximately 700,000, giving it one of the lowest population densities in the world. This population is divided into over a dozen tribes with almost as many languages, each with its own customs, traditions and beliefs. All depend on their animals for milk and meat. Cattle, sheep and goats, donkeys and camels are all important, although cows cannot survive in the harshest areas.

The north and east, towards Somalia and the settlements of Garissa and Wajir, is rather monotonous and flat but the whole of the north-west is hilly—in some parts mountainous—creating a stimulating wide-open landscape. It is a country which invites journeys for there is always a beckoning peak in the far distance.

Isolated in this vast desert area is Lake Turkana—160 miles long and the largest alkaline lake in the world. On the east side of the lake is the new Sibiloi National Park where there are enormous numbers of crocodiles and a good population of dry country plains game. Further south, Mount Marsabit has a National Reserve famous for its large elephant whilst on the southern edge of the dry country Samburu Game Reserve is one of the best known sanctuaries in Kenya.

Many visitors to the north of Kenya travel by light aircraft to Marsabit or one of the fishing lodges on Lake Turkana. But to get a real impression of the country one must travel overland. There are no tarmac roads in the whole of this area but all-weather roads have been made to Marsabit and the west side of Lake Turkana. Elsewhere it is wise to have a four-wheel drive vehicle and be completely self-contained.

On the rare occasions when it does rain the storms are heavy, so that the whole annual rainfall may come in just one or two torrential downpours. Flash floods then make rivers impassable and it might be necessary to wait for a swollen stream to go down before attempting a crossing.

The most popular journey in northern Kenya is to drive through Maralal and South Horr to Loiengalani on the east shores of Lake Turkana. The return is across the Chalbi Desert to Marsabit and then across the Kaisut Desert to Isiolo and Nairobi. This makes a round trip of 1,100 miles and it is a great mistake to hurry a safari of this type which can become very hard work indeed unless it is broken into sections. It is a good idea to spend several nights at each stop on the route and get to know something of each area. Maralal, Loiengalani and Marsabit are all good centres where the scenery, people and wildlife are more than rewarding.

Another worth-while trip is to the west side of Lake Turkana via the Kerio Valley and Lodwar. The southern part of this route is particularly beautiful with the Cherangani Hills dropping dramatically to the valley floor.

For some people northern Kenya becomes a strong magnet drawing them back again and again to explore the almost unknown corners away from the few main routes. Here one can wander over the hills and across the desert plains enjoying the scenery and isolation without seeing another vehicle for days.

Perhaps the best way of all for travel in this country is to go on foot but this must be properly organised as a small expedition.

The temperatures can be high in northern Kenya, 110°F in the shade being common. But the humidity is usually very low and there is often a hot, dry wind so that the sweat dries instantly and the climate is not uncomfortable. Water is obviously a problem and no one should embark on a journey without an adequate supply. Much of the region is stony desert where the roads can be very rough but there are other sections of dry, hard sand where driving is a pleasure.

The nomadic peoples of northern Kenya conservatively cling to their traditional life styles which are lived at a slow pace. Between themselves they are dignified and courteous and they appreciate good manners on the part of visitors.

In spite of the harsh nature of the country there are still good numbers of wild animals in northern Kenya. Some attractive species such as the Reticulated Giraffe and Beisa Oryx are only found in the northern half of Kenya. Grevy's Zebra, far more attractive than the Common Zebras of southern Kenya, are another feature of the north and can still be seen in a number of areas outside the reserves. Unfortunately their larger size and beautiful markings make them prime targets for the poachers and their numbers are reduced. But in any casual journey through northern Kenya many wild animals will be seen without being searched for. It is, perhaps, the combination of wildlife, traditional ways and spectacular scenery which gives the area its unique attraction.

A young Samburu moran. The Samburu speak the same language as the Masai and have many of the same customs.

THE SEMI-DESERT country which makes up the northern half of Kenya is still known by its old, romantic name, the Northern Frontier District, a name which symbolises the difference from the rest of the country.

If you drive into the N.F.D., no matter which route you take, there will come a point on your journey when suddenly the ground drops away to a distant shimmering plain. Here, infinite perspectives pull the eyes to the horizon, where peak after peak rises up out of the desert. Descending the escarpment, going down into the dry country, watching the dust-devils snake across the land, I have always had a feeling of commitment. One is conscious of entering a world with its own rules and disciplines, its own scales of time and distance.

The land area of the N.F.D. is larger than the whole of Great Britain, greater than Italy, six times as big as Holland, three times that of Portugal, bigger than Ghana or New Zealand. In the whole of this huge tract of country there are no tarmac roads and the sense of space is overwhelming. The average rainfall is under ten inches a year, and yet it contains a lake longer than Wales, numerous mountains topped with forest, several National Parks, vast numbers of wild animals and a population of about 700,000 pastoral, nomadic people.

The first Europeans to penetrate this area were Count Teleki and von Hönel who, in 1888, reached the huge lake then known as Basso Narok. This proved to be the largest alkaline lake in the world and Teleki renamed it Lake Rudolf after Prince Rudolf of Austria. Recently it has been renamed yet again, this time Lake Turkana, after the people who live on its southern and western shores.

Teleki went beyond Lake Turkana to Lake Stefanie, which in his time was an immense achievement involving an 800-mile walk from Mombasa, the last stretch being through stony and waterless desert.

Nowadays many people fly to Lake Turkana, hoping for a sense of adventure in comfort. But the only way to get the feel of this country is to travel overland and camp in it, soaking up the heat, the dust and the beauty, and staying long enough to make some kind of contact with the people. A journey through the N.F.D. is so full of stimulation that the minor discomforts— inevitable in a remote region with shade temperatures of up to 110°F—are more than amply repaid.

One returns with enlarged perspectives, the mind stretched by the spaciousness of the country and the glimpses of other ways of life so vastly different from our own.

On one trip I camped with friends under acacia thorns by a stream which tinkled down the mountain slopes above our tents only to go underground on the valley floor. First light one morning found us driving on a track which carries a vehicle two or three times a year.

Only an hour after dawn the sun already strikes with heat; the grass and low bush are burnt grey after months without rain. We bump across the empty plain; two miles back we saw zebra but here there is nothing, only the infinite perspectives framed by hills. We breast a rise and drop towards a lugga; suddenly the

landscape is full of camels, hundreds of them on the move, the air full of their bellowing voices, the sound of the wooden bells and the cries of the men, long-striding, spear-carrying, magnificently masculine. Rendille people, they move fast, soon fading into the immense distance.

To make the best use of the country they must move the camels up to forty miles a day, looking for new bush for browse, going perhaps for two weeks without water, rewarded by the milk of the camels which can give up to three times that of a cow. Only the young men in the tribe can maintain this kind of pace and so a Rendille family will normally divide its herd, retaining one to feed the women, children and older people, and sending off the other with the young men, who carry a heavy burden of responsibility, for camels are difficult to keep; and, because of the long period of gestation and large interval between pregnancies, it is hard to build up a camel herd if there are any losses.

The Samburu, who are the traditional allies of the Rendille, also divide their herds and send off one with the young men, but for very different reasons. The Samburu keep cows, not camels, and since cows eat grass and camels eat bushes the Rendille and Samburu live side by side in some areas. Cows cannot cover anything like the same distance as camels, nor can they go without water for more than a few days, and so looking after cows is physically easier. Indeed older men can manage cows perfectly well and there is a difference here in the method of watering the animals. In this region there is no surface water for more than two or three weeks after rain and so waterholes must be dug in the dry river beds. When the river first goes dry a hole six feet deep may suffice, but as the drought continues it must be enlarged and deepened, sometimes to a depth of more than thirty feet. Then water will be lifted by a chain of men working to the rhythm of a song, filled containers passed up with one hand, empty ones passed down with the other. To water a hundred animals will be a few hours' work and the animals themselves must be carefully controlled; the waterholes are fenced with thorns to prevent the stock from fouling them and the water is baled into a trough from which the animals drink. In Samburu society it is the older man who supervises his herd at the trough; the Rendille instead give this work to the younger men who thus have a higher place in their own society than their contemporary friends, the Samburu Moran.

The Moran of the pastoral nomadic tribes is a glamorous symbol of manhood throughout East Africa. But in Samburu society at least he exists more for the benefit of the elders than his own. True he has privileges: he may have affairs with unmarried girls (although he must not make them pregnant), he may dance and roam the countryside and even today many indulge in stock raids; he may dress himself up to emphasise his manhood. And yet he is an outcast from his society without responsibility in it.

Crossing the Chalbi Desert in northern Kenya. In the distance a small volcanic hill floats in a mirage and provides the only feature in an infinite landscape.

Turkana women returning home with head loads of wild roots. Being nomads they construct simple dwellings which they dismantle and carry with them on their wanderings. A termite nest towers above the middle hut.

Living away from the main family, looking after the surplus herd is more of a banishment than the necessity which it is with the camel-herding Rendille. He can even get away with irresponsibility more easily than the Rendille since, if he neglects the surplus herd, it is much easier to breed more cows than it is to increase a herd of camels. The Samburu Moran may not eat meat which has been seen by a married woman, may not drink milk inside a settlement unless accompanied by a fellow Moran; and of course he may not marry until he becomes an elder, which will be after a series of 'Ilmugit' ceremonies spread over a period of years. He is unlikely to marry until he is thirty and so this system makes it possible for the elders to have several wives. The Rendille, who marry younger and have a more responsible youth (there are no Rendille Moran), rarely have more than one wife, whereas by the time they are forty most Samburu men have two.

Naturally the Samburu Moran resent these restrictions and their own hopes of eventual marriage and success only partially contain their feelings. And yet, when one meets these people, the overwhelming effect is one of friendliness and cheerfulness. They seem so at one with their harsh environment, such a happy people, that one wonders how the tensions of the Moran are contained. This is done through the intricacies of the Samburu age-set system, aided by a belief in the power of the elders, the cultivation of respect as a high moral value and the strong psychological effect of the ceremonial side of life.

Psychologists have known for some time that people are more susceptible to new ideas when in a state of anxiety. The Samburu social system makes use of this facet of man's make-up at each of the Ilmugit ceremonies which take the Junior Moran gradually to elderhood and finally to marriage. Before each ceremony tension builds up because of everyone's desire that members of their own family should behave properly. Even for the circumcision ceremony there is more fear of failing to behave correctly than of the physical pain involved. This great anxiety of the participants enables them to accept their new role in society in a relatively unquestioning way.

Another aid to stability in Samburu society is the way in which the age-set system is organised. A new age-set will be created about once every dozen years and will comprise all the youths who have been circumcised during that period. Thus at any time there are living representatives of around six or seven age-sets, with a special relationship between alternate age-sets. When the new age-set is created and becomes the Junior Moran, a ceremony is performed where fire is kindled by the alternate age-set two up the scale. This more senior age-set now becomes the 'Firestick Elders' for the Junior Moran and are responsible for their education and discipline throughout their Moranhood. The power of the Firestick Elders is assured by the importance given to the idea of respect from a very early age. Respect should be shown to all the elders and to one's peers; selfish behaviour implies a lack of respect and so this concept has strong moral effects on the society.

Since the Samburu will not allow a gap of less than three age-sets between father and son, no man can be a Firestick Elder for his own son and so is relieved from the task of disciplining his own

This young man is a Turkana moran. His elaborate coiffure is formed with clay, usually painted blue; a bent reed gives a final touch of elegance. Being Nilo-Hamitic the Turkana do not practice circumcision, but boys still enter manhood through a series of initiation ceremonies during which two teeth are removed from the lower jaw.

Left:
Age, poverty and blindness have
failed to rob this Samburu woman
of her dignity.

Right:
This young woman has the
leather skirt, lip plug and blue
beads typical of the Turkana. The
cicatrice body decorations are
popular amongst the dry country
people who claim they make the
sexual act more interesting.

male children. Thus good feeling and stability in the family are safeguarded.

Is this perhaps why the Samburu seem so much more cheerful and friendly than the more dour and taciturn Turkana?

The Turkana are the traditional enemies of both the Rendille and the Samburu, a rivalry which is probably exacerbated by the fact that the Turkana own both cattle and camels and so come into direct competition with both the other tribes. In his account of Count Teleki's expedition von Hönel describes coming on a pile of two hundred camel skeletons near the east side of Lake Rudolf—now Lake Turkana. These turned out to be the result of a Turkana raid upon the Rendille. Since the Rendille were coming up on them at night the Turkana speared the stolen camels before escaping. Nowadays in several parts of Kenya Turkana, Samburu and Rendille may be seen living alongside each other, sometimes using the same waterholes, observing a truce imposed by modern administration.

In spite of the similarities of their ways of life there are obvious differences between them in their physical appearance and ways of dress. No less striking than his Samburu counterpart, there is no mistaking the Turkana with his darker skin and his elaborate coiffure of matted hair, dyed blue, which he protects at night by the use of a neck stool.

A pretty Samburu girl.

Looking across the Great Rift Valley from Maralal Mountain.

He too will be unable to marry until he is about thirty years old but since he is not restrained by the same age-set system he is in direct competition with his father. For the Turkana the marriage ceremony is of overwhelming importance. It is characteristic of all these tribes that animals, particularly the more important camels and cows, are an integral part of all their ceremonies. Animals are their only wealth, for they regard land and water as communal property: a striking contrast to the land-hungry agricultural tribes further south. The animals give milk, blood and meat; their skins give clothing, ornaments, sandals; gourds for milk and water; leather sleeping mats, thongs, snuff boxes and purses. And the dung makes fire and a roofing material. Animals are wealth; and to symbolise the importance of marriage the Turkana suitor must give around fifty camels and cows with perhaps one hundred goats and sheep to the bride's family. This large number of animals (which is about fourteen times the

A group of Gabbra nomads migrating across the Dida Galgalu—the Plain of Darkness—in the extreme north of Kenya. The curved sticks on the camels are the frameworks for their houses; chickens, puppies and children shelter amongst water-containers and cooking vessels under the canopies.

number of large stock per head of population) is a tremendous burden and compares with the Samburu bridewealth of only six or eight cows (which is about half the number of cows per head of population).

To raise the bridewealth a Turkana must increase his own herd and collect from his brothers, cousins, uncles and other close relatives. This takes a long time and much effort. Many of his relatives live at a distance so that he may have to walk over a hundred miles to acquire a single animal. It is largely the difficulty of collecting the necessary herd which delays the marriage of the Turkana. And, since there is a higher incidence of polygamy amongst the Turkana than the Samburu, in all this a young man will be in direct competition with his father and his own brothers. Thus tensions develop between father and son, and between brothers, which do not exist in Samburu society. However, the standing of wives is much higher amongst the

A Gabbra youth loading water on to his camel at a
well in the Chalbi Desert.

Turkana. When his wife's sisters marry he will receive some of the animals which are offered for them and so regain something of the sacrifice he has made. Because a young man is forced to break away from his father, ideas of independence and competition are much more prominent amongst the Turkana. But tensions are greater than among the Samburu who seem to be the happier people.

Any substantial journey through the N.F.D. brings contact with several tribes each of which has evolved its own unique way of achieving a stable way of life. Like interference in the natural world any disturbance of the established order can injure this stability so that often well-meaning acts can do harm. For example, the creation of a borehole may encourage people to stay after all the grazing is finished. They should move on to a new area where they will always be able to dig for water—indeed it is grazing not water which is the real shortage. If instead they cling

This Turkana man has been gathering wild gourds for use as water containers. He carries a neck stool, used as a pillow, to protect his coiffure.

to the comfort of the easy water of the borehole the animals can destroy the root system within two days' march around it; when the rains come there will be no new growth.

One wonders what the children will learn in the schools established by the missions and others which will help them to survive in this arid country. Up to the present these schools are distressingly conventional, aiming to provide an education suitable for a suburban child rather than a desert dweller. At best this will remove the more gifted individuals from the society and send them to the towns. At worst it will teach them to question the traditional methods and values of their societies without offering them a viable alternative. Even medical and veterinary services create problems by adding to the growth of population which these areas simply cannot support. Irrigation might help in some areas; but again, if water is used more rapidly than the natural rate at which the underground reserves are replenished, a temporary expedient would cause a future disaster. In the past, periodic droughts and famines have controlled both the human and animal populations. Now, relief, aid and medicine prevent such disasters from having the same effects. Will this enormous improvement in the life of the individuals concerned have to be paid for by the destruction of their societies? By the time the societies themselves are sufficiently aware of what is happening it will be too late for them to turn back and the world will be left with the same sense of regret which has been expressed for the bushmen, the eskimos, the natives of Tahiti.

This is not to argue that the pastoral nomad's traditional way of life is ideal in arid areas for this is clearly not the case. The reliance which the nomads place on milk means they need large numbers of animals which inevitably damage the environment by overgrazing. On the other hand the fact that the people of these areas are nomadic is very probably a virtue as this gives an area time to regenerate. Only nature herself really knows how to exploit this kind of country, for the vast range of natural species makes far more efficient use of the available vegetation than man's four or five domestic animals; and nature is certainly in favour of nomadic species.

The most likely hope for the pastoral peoples is to persuade them to sell a proportion of their stock each year as meat and use the cash to buy grain. In this way they would need less animals and so could have a more secure existence without damaging the already fragile environment. Some work along these lines is being done, but not enough, and unfortunately most of the help being offered now does not touch this fundamental problem.

At Kargi, in Rendille country on the edge of the Koroli Desert, I met the local Chief who is responsible to the District Commissioner for controlling his area. He showed me the skin of a male lion which had been shot a few days previously after it had killed three camels and he told me that last year thirteen lions were shot in Kargi. Life is still very hard in this area and the Chief was full of praise for the work of the missionaries. I have met many of the missionaries working in Northern Kenya and I admire them; but I often wonder whether their efforts to help the desert nomads really succeed or whether they just create new problems.

Cactus flowers make a splash of colour in hot, dry areas.

A Samburu woman with her leather water bottles
in a dried-out river-bed where she can still find
water by digging below the surface. In northern
Kenya the real shortage is good grazing. Water is
always available if you dig for it.

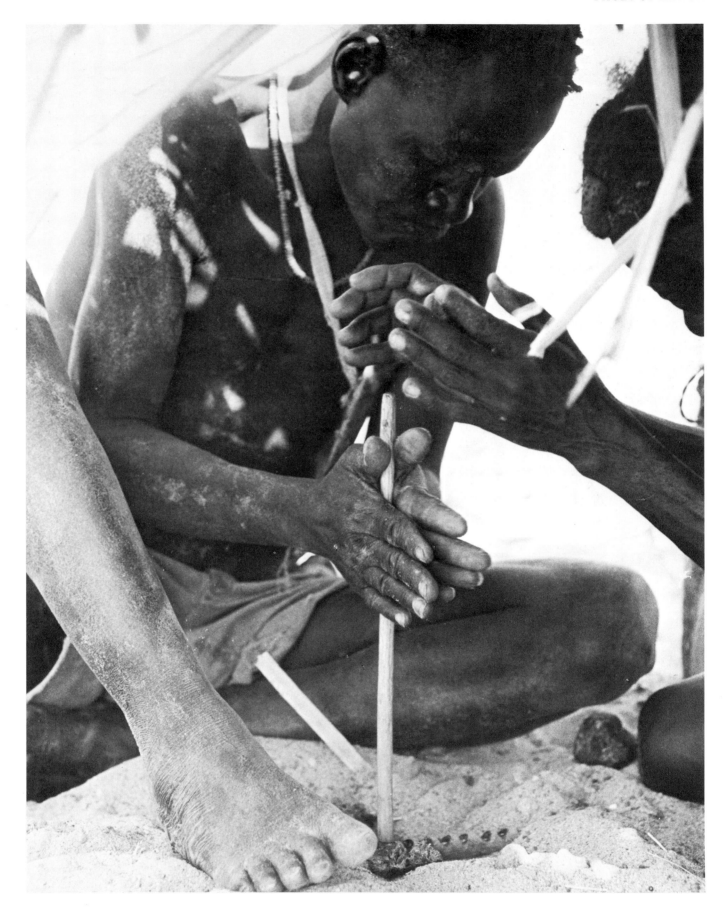

Many of the desert peoples of northern Kenya preserve the art of making fire, although it is rare to be able to photograph it. These two men had a fire going within five minutes, using special pieces of wood which they carry with them as we might carry a lighter.

The Chief at Kargi has a small house of metal sheets with no windows which was surprisingly cool inside. There were three wooden chairs in the house and pictures of Italy carefully glued to the corrugated iron walls. The Chief has been to Italy and he says it is the Catholic Mission which is really giving them hope by sending the children to school. The school is boarding and the mission collects the children in a lorry each term, thus overcoming the usual problem with nomadic people.

I expressed my doubts about all this and asked the Chief, 'What happens when children finish at school? Don't they find it difficult to rejoin their families?'

He replied 'Of course, yes. If possible they try to go on to secondary, technical, or some other training.'

'And what about those who fail to go further? Do they accept a return to the nomadic way of life?'

'They find it very difficult. Some become rascals; some try to go to Nairobi.'

'What will happen in, say, fifteen years when all the children have been to school? Won't there be a serious problem then?'

'That is true; it will be a very great problem.'

'How do you think we can solve this problem?'

'That we don't know. But we must try to think about it.'

'In the old days an intelligent man, who today might succeed in secondary school, would be of great value in his community and become a leader. Nowadays he will be lost to the community

This Boran woman is repairing a large kibuyu—water carrier—typically carried on a camel. Raffia from palm fronds, dried mud and dung are used to construct these finely made vessels which last many years.

and so the community will be gradually weakened. Does this make life harder for those left behind?'

'Yes; but we must try to overcome this. In any case education is the hope here and the Mission are very good for they will even pay the school fees for someone who does not have the ability to pay.'

What the missionaries are teaching the Rendille that will help them to live more easily in the desert is not clear and the tragedy is that medical and veterinary care increase both human and stock populations beyond the carrying capacities of these marginal lands. I fear that education is breaking up the stable social systems of the pastoral tribes without touching on the main necessity, which is to find a way of living in semi-desert without turning it into full desert. To my mind all the effort now being put into schools should be redirected on to this fundamental problem.

In some areas the Samburu build their houses on stilts. They say this protects them from mosquitoes.

A Gabbra woman moving house. The camel is carrying all her possessions—everything she needs for survival in the semi-desert of northern Kenya. The sticks will form the framework of her house; her baby shelters under the canopy with the mats, chickens and gourds.

Meanwhile, for travellers, there is still the possibility of observing the desert people before they change too much.

Many visitors make a trip to Lake Turkana in order to give their journey some kind of focus in the midst of the vast emptiness. The journey to the west side of the lake is easier and shorter; on this side of the lake one meets Pokot people, who have been irrigating their land on the edge of the Cherangani Hills since long before the first white man reached their country, and further north the Turkana.

A journey to the east side of the lake is longer and more difficult and also more rewarding. Here one will meet Samburu, Turkana, Rendille and, at the lake itself, the El Molo—the impoverished ones—a tiny tribe who live by fishing and spearing crocodile and turtle. The mission at Loiengalani was founded to help this tribe and there is now a mixed encampment of El Molo and Samburu living in small low dwellings of dried palm leaves; inside they have the cosiness of nests but their main function is to keep off the sun and wind. The wind is a schizophrenic friend on the east side of the lake, at once threatening and making life tolerable.

All night long a gale rushes through the open tent; bodying canvas and thrashing palms fill the travelling air with noise and in the breaks of sleep one steps outside to soak in the jet black sky, sown with diamonds. Morning brings a purist dawn with a continuing infinity of rushing air, hot and dry, tearing off the desert, drying the sweat instantly, hurrying to the lake where it chases white horses to the western horizon. There is a fascination, almost a madness, in the settlement at Loiengalani where life clings to an oasis of pure spring water which emerges from the earth at 120°F to succour palms and men, camels and safari lodge, even the missionaries' lettuces. The thermometer registers 110°F in the shade but the unceasing wind compensates and one is free to enjoy the people, the flamingoes and the pelicans, and to wonder at the immensity of the lake set in the yet more immense desert.

Crossing the desert is one of the main features of a journey to the east side of Lake Turkana. One leaves the lake over stony ground with steep ascents and fields of lava boulders; then comes the Chalbi Desert, a huge expanse of sun-baked sand, featureless but for a floating mountain, detached from the earth, marking the way to North Horr. One must drive off the road into the trackless sand and stop to savour the emptiness. Really to get the feel of it, walk a hundred yards from the Landrover and try to grasp the huge shimmering perspectives. Only the horizon imprisons here; to escape requires either a track or a compass. The distances dominate and fascinate the mind as the board of sand rolls under the wheels for hours. The vehicle drones away on an infinite plane surrounded by mirages which disappear when one stops and climbs on the roof. In parts the desert is caked with salt as dazzling as a dusting of snow and here, out of sight of vegetation of any kind, I have seen Grant's Gazelle and ostrich.

Around the Chalbi Desert one may also meet Gabbra and Boran people. Both tribes keep camels and live in this immensely difficult country. The Boran and Gabbra women are the only tribes in Kenya habitually to wear their hair long; with their slim

This elegant Turkana woman is carrying a gourd of water home from a well. The small gourd contains milk.

bones and fine features many of them have a striking beauty. In spite of their tough life the Boran are a cheerful and friendly people. When a family migrates to find a new browse for their animals everything is carried on the camels. Pots, gourds, mats, skins, chickens, all are lashed on. The babies are cradled in the midst of these household possessions above which tower the curved frames of the dwellings, draped with cloth to shade the children. To see a line of these loaded camels strung out across the desert, the bent sticks nodding above like huge birds, a symbolic human figure guiding the leading camel, is to behold something so out of time it is not merely biblical, but pre-biblical.

It is salutary to reflect that in this country these people are rich, for here to possess camels is to possess wealth. Indeed there are desert families who have a capital value tied up in animals which will exceed the total assets of some misguided visitors who pity them. To find really poor people you must go to the extreme north-east of Lake Turkana beyond the new National Park, which contains the world's last big concentration of crocodile feeding on the abundant fish of this enormous brackish lake. Here, there are little groups of men, without animals or possessions of any kind who have turned to the lake for a bare existence. Being totally poor they have no wives and live in tight units of friendship and mutual dependence. They, like the El Molo, fish the lake, spear crocodiles and turtles. These are the hunter-gatherers, living totally outside the modern world, making fire with two pieces of wood, preserving independence by simply doing without what they cannot create for themselves. Incredibly, they too seem happy.

It is poetically appropriate that palaentologists should now be excavating some of the oldest human skulls yet known in this remote part of northern Kenya. For today in this dry country there survive a variety of social systems which, arduous though they are, should open our eyes to values which exist outside the enclosed technological world in which most of us now find ourselves.

In the game parks, wonderful as they are, there is a feeling of falseness; one of the important mammals is missing. Up in the northern desert country the people, as well as the animals, are in their natural environment and one can glimpse a way of life that has already survived a number of millennia.

It is probable that the missions, the air strips and the dukas, the doctors, the government officers and the tourists will gradually erode this ancient but living monument to man's strength and versatility. And yet, seeing them side by side at some desert outpost like North Horr, it is the modern world which looks more fragile. Is it really too sentimental to think that, when our civilisation has joined the Romans', the beautiful Boran people will still be striding, with their camels, across the great, dry spaces of the world?

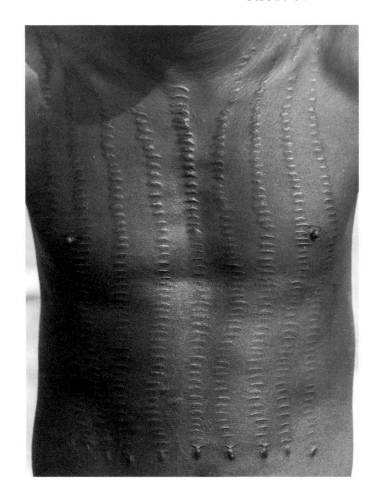

Throughout northern Kenya many people admire
cicatrice body decorations. This exceptional
example is proudly worn by a Shankilla man.

A herd of camels leaving Lake Turkana.

Left:
Only babies ride on camels in Kenya. Even young children are expected to walk long distances.

A Rendille youth with his bell camel that leads a large herd.

This large group of camels have just been watered at Lake Turkana.
Now they will move into the hills to browse; the milk of these camels
is the staple diet of their Turkana owners.

Left:
A woman of Marsabit.

Right:
A Turkana woman and her baby.

Left
A Samburu woman.

Right
A Rendille youth watering camels at an ancient well. Water is baled into a hollowed log using a bucket made of giraffe hide.

Left:
This young Pokot woman is going through her
period of initiation. For five months after
circumcision there must be no contact with men;
this outfit is designed to remove temptation.

A Gabbra mother with her baby at North Horr.

A Samburu man playing the ancient game of bao
which is popular all over Kenya.

Right:
A young Boran woman outside her home.

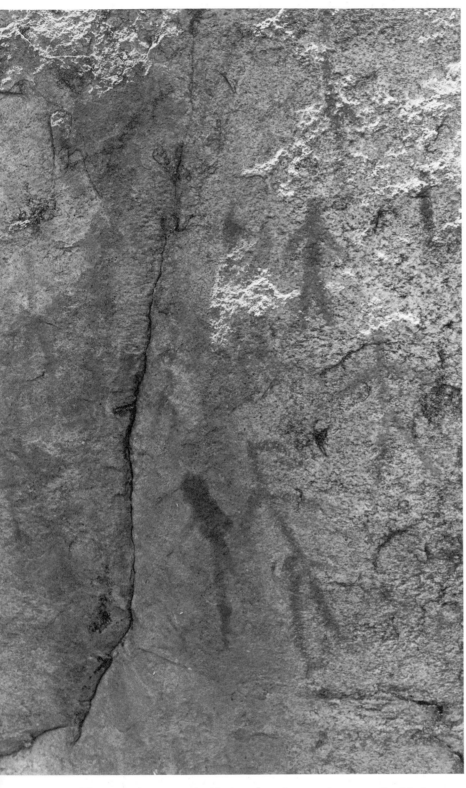

These very recent rock paintings are the work of Samburu men who say they do them for fun.

A stony desert south of Lake Turkana where pieces of petrified wood 40 million years old may be found lying amongst the boulders.

Huge trunks of petrified wood near Alia Bay in the Sibiloi National Park, east of Lake Turkana. Radioactive dating gives an age of 40 million years for this cedar-like timber.

An old Boran man in a typical pose. Nomads in
many parts of Kenya will walk for hours with a
stick held thus.

This Boran man is wearing the traditional finery for the naming of his new-born son.

Overleaf:
Northern Kenya is, above all, a land of vast spaces. Here the road from Baragoi to South Horr turns to the east of the Nyiru Range which rises to 9,030 ft 25 miles from Lake Turkana.